THE
PSYCHOLOGY
OF
CALL RELUCTANCE:

HOW TO OVERCOME THE FEAR OF SELF-PROMOTION

THE
PSYCHOLOGY
OF
CALL RELUCTANCE:

HOW TO OVERCOME THE FEAR OF SELF-PROMOTION

George W. Dudley
Shannon L. Goodson

BEHAVIORAL SCIENCE RESEARCH PRESS

Dallas
1986

Copyright © 1986 by Behavioral Science Research Press, Inc.

Published by Behavioral Science Research Press, Inc.
2695 Villa Creek Drive, Suite 100
Dallas, Texas 75234

Editorial Supervision and Inside Design by Gary E. Minnich
Cover Design by Bill Grosjean

10 9 8 7 6 5

Printed in the United States of America

Library of Congress Cataloging in Publication Data

Dudley, George W., 1943-
     The psychology of call reluctance.

     Includes index.
     1. Selling—Psychological aspects. 2. Telephone
selling—Psychological aspects. I. Goodson,
Shannon L., 1952-   . II. Title.
HF5438.8.P75D83 1985   658.8'5   85-73334
ISBN 0-935907-00-9
ISBN 0-935907-01-7 (pbk.)

This book is dedicated to the memory of Don M. Wolfe. A talented and caring salesman and sales manager, his insatiable curiosity and lively intellect was a credit to his profession. His optimistic encouragement and unselfish support brightened our early work with call reluctance and years later inspired the writing of this book.

CONTENTS

1

THE FACES OF CALL RELUCTANCE

2

THE PRESCRIPTIONS

3

THE RESEARCH

PREFACE

The pulsating beat of modern industry does not easily yield the time that is necessary to monitor advances in the behavioral sciences. Instead, business people must often wait for months and even years before benefiting from the fascinating theories and functional technologies spawned by this rich and broad scientific discipline. Typically, information from the behavioral sciences trickles into the business community only through speeches, books and cassettes produced by men and women who serve as self-appointed interpreters. Calling themselves motivation or performance experts, these interpreters seem to pop up in some industries like mushrooms pop up from the ground. Relying on information based on hearsay and informal sources like newspaper and magazine accounts, these interpreters are essentially entertainers. Few have the skill, background or interest to search out and read primary scientific source material themselves. The result is incomplete or misunderstood information passed on to uncritical business consumers as factual and representative. Due to faulty transmission, information capable of making dramatic differences in the way important considerations are managed, is watered down or garbled in transit. Nowhere is this more evident than in the management of the fear of self-promotion, or call reluctance (fear of self-promotion that interferes with the prospecting activity of sales-people). Some entire industries have failed to benefit from the modern technology available to manage call reluctance because they simply don't know it exists. And they don't know it exists because the source they use to keep them up-to-date and informed on such matters—their interpreters—also don't know it exists.

Recently, we had the opportunity to observe this futile and wasteful process at an industry convention. A consultant was speaking from the main platform about maximizing sales performance. Over the last 15 years of studying the fear of self-promotion, we have heard many such speeches. The patter and technique of this particular consultant were typical and predictable.

In our experience, there always seems to come a humorous point during call reluctance presentations when the speaker (we'll call him Tom) seems to have enough control over both subject and audience to bring time itself to a stand still. We can still recall how Tom did it. . .

The audience was filled with eager anticipation as the presentation neared its end. Everyone grew noticeably tense, like small children with a full bladder. Then Tom, radiating sincerity, unexpectedly stopped for emphasis. He grinned knowingly to himself, gazed off into the unfocused distance, closed his eyes, and contemplatively stroked his meticulously trimmed beard. He began to gesture as if something really momentous was about to be said, which from all appearances was in the process of being providentially revealed to him. With pupils dilated with excitement, the audience waited for what seemed like an eternity. Tom then began to dispense mentalistic words of wisdom like amphetamines for confused and bewildered call reluctant spirits. "Remember, we've all experienced call reluctance," he said, lowering his voice to whispering solemnity. "Everybody has it. But," he continued, his words sharpening and his voice growing louder, "call reluctance is nothing more than the fear of rejection; and you can beat it if you'll just do three things for me: Learn to relax while you work, learn to laugh at yourself, and learn to distinguish between being turned down personally and just having your ideas turned down."

The audience applauded politely. Many looked disappointed. Some looked transfixed. The master of ceremonies rose to reclaim the microphone. "That's really heavy," he chanted reverently. "We've really struck some deep chords here today. I hope you all hear Tom's message because he really knows our heads. If we go back and share this with our sales force, we'll have the best year ever!"

Most of the audience left quickly. But a faithful few lingered worshipfully around Tom. Most were asking about his $250 per day Personal Performance Workshop. Tom was in rare form. Not a tall man, he stood as erect as he could to broadcast his "power gaze" and optimize his "command presence." He dropped names and slung out answers to questions with the speed and agility of a verbal food processor. One manager, a pop psych groupie, finally managed to get Tom's attention. Enraptured, he testified that his career had been scarred by the fear of rejection. But now he was completely restored. He could feel it. He knew it and "just had to share it with the group" (a phrasing we suspected he might have picked up during group psychotherapy). But this was obviously not this manager's first outing into pop psych matters. He had been there before. Many times. Maybe one too many times. Sporting an out-of-focus, thousand-mile stare and beaming a beatified smile, he looked to us like he had just swallowed a near fatal dose of Valium and couldn't remember how to change the expression on his face.

This feature plays daily. Millions of salespeople and their managers eat Mac Wisdom served up by Tom and other proprietors of the mental fast food industry. Tom's a heavy. But is he your brother?

If you have call reluctance or manage people who have it, he's not. The residue of faulty and incomplete information which he unintentionally leaves behind is one of the reasons that call reluctance remains the problem it is in some industries. Clamoring tightly together in a room to hear people like Tom brings to mind the medieval practice of crowding into churches to pray for delivery from the plague, thereby assuring its rapid and unhindered spread.

We, along with other behavioral scientists using sophisticated new research methods, have discovered the reasons for call reluctance. We have developed powerful new training procedures to neutralize it. Years of research, development and field testing are all included on the following pages. This is the first attempt to bring the bulk of our work on call reluctance directly to you. We hope you find it worthwhile and enjoyable.

George W. Dudley   Shannon L. Goodson

ACKNOWLEDGEMENTS

This book reflects the efforts and influences of many people. Our use and development of specialized tests was highly influenced by the mathematical approach to personality theory and measurement reflected in the work of R.B. Cattell and others who pioneered the modern, scientific study of personality. The prescriptions we developed for call reluctance carry influences from several distinct traditions in counseling and psychotherapy. Albert Ellis, Victor Frankl, Arnold Lazarus, Joseph Wolpe and other scientists developed the core concepts and procedures that we adapted and applied to fear of self-promotion performance problems and behaviors.

Carol A. Dudley deserves special commendation for assuming two roles. As a neuro-scientist, she refined our understanding of certain relevant brain functions. As the wife of one of the authors, she also patiently tolerated a trashed-out dining room during the years this book was being researched and written. Suzanne Dudley provided us encouragement and the opportunity to observe how an adolescent first learns to deal with the fear of self-promotion. Gloria Black, our administrative manager, insulated us from telephone calls and kept the office humming smoothly. Gary Minnich played an invaluable role. As editor and page designer, he made sure that scientific mumbo-jumbo ended up on the cutting room floor and that what made it to the printer was readable and attractively laid out. This book is also a tribute to the thousands of salespeople, managers, trainers and consultants who shared their call reluctance pains and frustrations with us over the years. They added a sorely needed human dimension to our heavy metal research. Last, we wish to thank ourselves. After years of working together on the fear of self-promotion, we were finally able to agree on enough points to write this book.

1

THE FACES
OF
CALL RELUCTANCE

The thick-skinned fearlessness expected in salespeople is more fiction than fact. It turns out that many salespeople are struggling with a bone-shaking fear of prospecting. This fear tends to persist regardless of what they sell, how well they have been trained to sell it, or how much they personally believe in the product's worth.

CHAPTER ONE

THE INVISIBLE MAN

THE WAY WE WERE

It's a typical Monday evening at the United Metro Insurance Agency. Nancy, an agent for three weeks, sits at her desk. Now and then she glances at a nearby wall clock. She knows that prospecting for new business is critical if she is to succeed in her new sales career. But that awareness is not enough to immunize her against an involuntary heart-pounding fear she can't understand or control.

The selection psychologist who interviews prospective agents for the United Metro Agency "strongly recommended" Nancy for a career in life insurance sales. The standard paper-and-pencil psychological test administered during the selection process awarded her its highest score. She has the personality, intelligence and motivation to succeed in sales. She has been armed with newly sharpened interpersonal skills, an array of aggressively competitive new products, access to expensive state-of-the-art portable computers, and expert support from the home office. But Nancy is like the caterpillar who said to the butterfly as it winged effortlessly overhead, "You'll never get *me* to go up in one of *those*." Though equipped by nature and nurtured for success in sales, prospecting scares her to death and keeps her career from ever getting off the ground.

But this time she is determined to get a sales appointment. So she draws a few deep self-assuring breaths and reaches for the first card from her prospect card file. "I know what to say and how to say it," she reminds herself. Then she dials the number. As the phone rings on the other end, her resolve strengthens but her composure weakens. Her breath rate increases, each breath becomes shallower than the one before. Her memory, usually saber sharp, becomes murky and clouded over. Struggling desperately to conceal her discomfort, she begins her presentation in a voice which is now barely audible. "Hello. My name is Nancy. . ."

Bob is another story. He's been an automobile salesman for four years. Everyone expected him to be a heavy hitter. And although his initial production did rise steadily, it soon leveled off on a disappointingly low plateau. Bob's sales manager sent him to a number of seminars and workshops. His attitude, never really a problem, has improved but his production has not; it remains frozen at a level considerably below his talent, market and ability.

Bob's dealership even sponsored an extensive market analysis to help its salespeople target additional prospects in an effort to help them limit their dependence upon floor traffic. But Bob refuses to make sales calls on some of his targets. Instead, he indignantly points out that some of his "so-called targets" are actually members of his own family. "*Real* salespeople," according to Bob, "never make calls on members of their own family."

Larry is a sales veteran. He has fought in the trenches selling computer products for several years. He's been in hardware/software sales since 1980. He is undeniably dedicated and extremely capable in every respect except one, *prospecting*. While he has changed over the years, he has not grown. His production remains at 1981 levels. Larry likes to boast that he can "sell anybody, anytime, anyplace," and he probably can unless they happen to be physicians, lawyers, accountants or other up-market professionals and decision makers. Unfortunately for Larry, these groups represent the prime market for his company's new line of computer products.

Larry has been asked, begged and ordered to direct his sales calls to the company's primary market. He can't or won't. He has been sent to psychiatrists, stress managers and the leading sales training seminars in his industry. He has listened to exhortations from motivational speakers, read inspirational books, and been taught how to establish *eye contact*. But he is still downsighted. He can only set his prospecting sights in one direction, *downward*. His overworked rebuttal is, "I don't make calls on *them* SOB's."

Willie Doesn't Live Here Any More

Just a few short years ago, salespeople were presumed to be male, outgoing and audacious. Times have changed. Women are discovering that sales positions can offer them the opportunity to go further and faster than non-sales positions. Sales training now teaches the salesperson that selling is a collaborative, need-centered negotiation. Products in many industries have become much more sophisticated, competitive and complex. But what about the stereotype? It remains intact.

In *Death of a Salesman*, Arthur Miller crafted an image of an anchorless drifter who was shiftless, self-interested and superficial. With Willie Loman's "smile and a shoeshine" character, Miller's fiction was projected onto the awareness of an entire culture. There his story blended into the popular mythology about salespeople until the two become indistinguishable. People began to believe that salespeople really were like Willie Loman.

A few decades ago, psychologists and psychiatrists, never at a loss for words themselves, began to speculate about the inner workings of this curious subspecies. Adjectives were shuffled about in wildly descriptive abandon as they celebrated their ritual dance of linguistic narcissism. Chanting complex and spooky incantations like "ambivalence," "sublimated drives" and "meta-motivation," they employed verbal sleight-of-hand to repackage the old stereotype into the new mentalistic language of the times. Much more light could have been shed on the subject if they had bumped their heads together and produced a small spark.

Here's an actual "thumbnail sketch" of the life insurance salesperson as seen through the eyes of a college level psychology textbook:

"Didn't choose occupation; stumbled into it.
Ambitious, desires success, money, luxuries.
Likes selling and business.
Dislikes aesthetic and scientific activities.
Aggressively hostile, sociable on a large scale.
Dependent on others for advice and companionship.
Conservative and authoritarian.
Sensitive to criticism.
Doer, rather than thinker.
May exploit others financially."

In their promotional material of a few years ago, two psychologists selling sales selection tests to industry characterized the desirable candidate for a sales career with these words:

"...friendly and outgoing, but when you know him he is arrogant, conceited and not very interested in people...but when he begins to talk he can be a most persuasive, charming, convincing individual . . . he gains your confidence and makes you feel like the most important person in the world . . . but don't be fooled, he doesn't really like people . . . to him people are just objects to be twisted, shaped and manipulated."

The picture that emerges is not that of innocent winged figures robed in dazzling white. It's more like mild retardates with probable criminal intent.

Are salespeople the oversocialized, fearless mercenaries they are made out to be? Superficial studies based on the stereotype above suggest so. And we have found that most current sales selection systems are biased in favor of the stereotype. For example, we found in a recent study that the most common trait measured in sales selection systems is high dominance (social forcefulness). The second most frequently reported trait is high sociability. But modern in-depth personality studies, which have probed beneath the surface that is usually only scratched by most sales selection tests, tell another story.

Our own studies have confirmed that salespeople vary considerably from their stereotypes. Armed with the newest state-of-the-art sales assessment systems, we found that salespeople as a group are barely distinguishable in terms of forcefulness and sociability from the general population of adults. Furthermore, the thick-skinned fearlessness expected in salespeople is more fiction than fact. It turns out that many salespeople are struggling with a bone-shaking fear of prospecting. This fear tends to persist regardless of what they sell, how well they have been trained to sell it, or how much they personally believe in the product's worth. The result is a lot of Nancys, Bobs and Larrys. You may know one. You may be one. Each has a disease peculiar to direct salespeople. Technically, it is called the *fear of self-promotion* because it interferes with the ability to promote one's interests in many different areas of life, not just in sales. But in sales, it cuts off the supply of vital new business at its source by interfering with the act of *prospecting*. When this happens, it is called *call reluctance*.

THE INVISIBLE MAN

In direct sales, results are critically linked to the number of contacts initiated with prospective buyers. Figures vary somewhat depending upon industry, product and skill, but most sales training directors agree that the relationship between new contacts and sales success is extremely important. Generally it takes about 25 contacts to get 12 responses which result in five real sales presentations and three closed sales. Most salespeople know this. But legions of otherwise capable salespeople fail each year because they are unable or unwilling to translate what they *know* about prospecting into prospecting *behavior*.

Our studies show that as many as 80% of all salespeople who fail within their first year do so because of insufficient prospecting activity.

What about veteran salespeople? Our research shows that during their careers, approximately 40% of them will experience one or more episodes of call reluctance severe enough to threaten their continued tenure in sales. Experience does not immunize.

Call reluctance is a career-threatening condition which limits what salespeople can achieve by emotionally limiting the number of sales calls they are able to make. Some have trouble using the phone as a prospecting tool. Others have trouble initiating face-to-face contact with prospective buyers. Some have trouble doing both.

Can Phone Machines Circumvent Call Reluctance?

Got call reluctance? Maybe the ever-present micro chip can help. It promises leads without having to personally prospect. So say the mobs of hard-wired, auto dialing computer prospectors. Aside from the growing social disapproval over their use, can they be an effective prospecting surrogate?

One sales manager thought so. Perplexed and disappointed by the call reluctance plaguing the human element of his sales force, he waited impatiently for the arrival of his first non-human addition. Costing in dollars much more than it weighed in pounds, it came with the promise that it would not—*could* not—ever become call reluctant. That's what the manager wanted to hear. That's why he bought it.

But in the realm of human action, dreams of highly improved production can be highly perishable. And they were. Three things happened. First, the leads that the machine produced were inconsistent with his market. Second, the quality of the business he realized from the leads was not what he had envisioned. It was poor both in terms of the dollar amount per sale and the length of time it remained on the books.

But it was the third point which became the most perplexing. Although the overall number of leads did increase, the number of follow-up sales calls made by his human sales force remained about the same. It seems that our manager overlooked a very basic point. Arguably, machines may be able to generate leads, but in direct sales, people still have to sell. His people couldn't make prospecting calls before the machine, and they couldn't make follow-up calls after it. The machine was sold after one month of use.

The fear of self-promotion is the general condition behind call reluctance in salespeople. It is found in motivated, goal-striving people everywhere who have great emotional difficulty promoting themselves. Not limited to salespeople alone, it keeps competent and deserving people in almost every walk of life from being recognized for their contributions and, therefore, from getting ahead.

Too modest to "toot his own horn," a loyal and deserving administrator is not promoted to the next higher position because someone less competent, but more visible, gets the job.

Sacrificially modest about her contributions, a hard working partner in an accounting firm does not get the end-of-year performance bonus she deserves because another partner, less capable than her, sensed her vulnerability and took credit for some of her accomplishments. The fear of self-promotion can make you *invisible.*

People who fear self-promotion tend to be dreamers. Tucked away with the fairy tales and fables of their childhood are innocent expectations they bring with them to their careers. These are not realistic representations of the way things are, but rather the romantic idealizations of what could be if men were angels. But they're not.

These idealistic myths fall into two basic groups, fallacies of reward and fallacies of recognition. Some of them are as follows.

Idealistic Myth: If you are loyal to your superiors, you can trust them to look out for your welfare.

Practical Reality: You are responsible for *yourself.* It's not your superior's job to take care of you or your career. Loyalty is nice, but not symmetric. Just because you choose to be loyal does not mean that others have to be loyal to your interests. Don't be disappointed when you find they are not. It is reasonable to expect your company, its owners and its management *to look after their own interests first.*

Idealistic Myth: The hardest working, best producing and most deserving people always eventually rise to the top.

Practical Reality: Open your eyes. Look around. Are the individuals at the top of your organization *necessarily* the most competent? People who are *perceived* to be the most competent are the ones who typically make it to the top. But they cannot be perceived as competent if their competency is invisible. Getting to the top of any enterprise or organization you don't own requires a two-part approach: competent performance packaged in assertive self-promotion. Competent performance without assertive self-promotion is a dead end.

Idealistic Myth: Good work speaks for itself.

Practical Reality: Work gets rewarded from only two basic sources. One is the personal satisfaction and feeling of accomplishment you award yourself when you know you have done your job well. That's important but it is also very private. The other is the public recognition and financial reward you get from doing your job well. This source is based on the behaviors of others and it lies mostly outside the realm of your control. Its payoffs can be meaningful. But since they are calculated by *other* people who are trying to be good expense managers or shrewd corporate navigators in order to *maximize their own rewards,* the payoffs for *your* good work are likely to be as insignificant and infrequent as *you* will allow.

Ethical Self-Promotion

To some people, any kind of self-promotion is unethical. It's a contradiction, like the term "round square." While self-promotion *can* be unethical, it doesn't have to be. It can be healthy, rewarding and even fun. Ethical self-promotion is based on the realistic necessity and mature understanding that success in *any* contact-dependent endeavor requires both effective performance and effective self-promotion. But ethical self-promotion takes one additional step. It is a *balanced* chemistry of self-promotional activities combined with sensitivity and respect for the needs and rights of other people.

There are many sources which claim to be able to teach the mechanics of self-promotion. Most of them sound the same. In our judgement, however, one stands out above the others. It's called *The Unabashed Self-Promoter's Guide* by Dr. Jeffrey Lant. We regularly recommend it to dentists, psychologists, lawyers, salespeople and others whose success depends upon the quality and frequency of their contacts with other people. If you don't know how to effectively make contact with large numbers of prospective buyers, it can teach you. But for most, knowing *how* is not the critical factor. Being emotionally *able* is.

THE FIVE ORIGINS OF CALL RELUCTANCE

Call reluctance results in career-limiting behaviors. But what is a behavior? There are many explanations derived from various behavioral models. Everybody has a model. Needless to say, they do not all agree.

Other Behavioral Models

Behavior has been modeled by many sources before and since the advent of modern behavioral science. Here's a sampling of some representative alternative explanations for your call reluctant behavior.

Religious:	Devil made you do it
Cosmic:	Position of celestial bodies at the time of your birth
Environmental:	Shaped by rewards and punishments
Chemical:	Emotional footprints left by chemical events in your brain

---

Don't *All* Salespeople Have Call Reluctance?

Don't all salespeople have call reluctance? Yes and no. Actually, the notion that all salespeople have call reluctance is a popular misconception which is based upon an imprecise definition of what call reluctance is. All salespeople may have a *predisposition* to one or more *forms* of call reluctance, but that does not mean they *have* it. We also have microorganisms in our bloodstreams which predispose us, under certain conditions, to an uninvited bout with the flu. But while the genesis of the illness may be present at any given time, the actual debilitating symptoms we associate with the flu are not.

To decrease the likelihood of getting the flu, or limit its severity if it should occur, health conscious people take vitamins, live healthy lifestyles, and have flu shots prior to the flu season. Call reluctance can be prevented in the same way. Even if you do not have the symptoms of call reluctance at the present time, you can learn what types you are most predisposed to and then apply the precautionary steps provided for you later in this book. Think of it as your immunization against the call reluctance season of your sales career.

Pop psych groupies will probably find that the behavioral model we use lacks sex appeal. Consultants and graduate students will find it altogether too unmysterious to describe in their low, churchly voices. But we use it because it is, as Professor J.R. Haynes, Chairman of the Department of Psychology at North Texas State University, likes to say, "simple, straightforward and self-evident." More than that, our model also provides the jumping off point for our corrective assaults later on.

Whatever else a behavior may be, it can be reduced to at least three elements: *thoughts, feelings,* and *actions.* Everything you *do* (actions) is accompanied by thoughts and feelings. They may all be related in some complex fashion, and then again they may not be. Despite what you read elsewhere, no one knows for sure. The evidence is incomplete. The jury is still out. But we do know that call reluctance in salespeople is a problem which usually involves exaggerated feelings and can also involve all three elements of behavior.

Where does call reluctance come from? Its origins are multiple and complex. There is no single source, no single "germ" to isolate and destroy. A few forms clearly result from hereditary predispositions. Others have been traced back to traumatic early selling experiences. Often it is precipitated by extremely high performance pressures. Ironically, it is often unintentionally taught by the sales training process itself. It can be present at the outset of the career, or it can strike years later without warning or apparent justification.

The genealogy of any behavior, including the fear of self-promotion, can be traced to one or more of the following origins. Knowing where call reluctance comes from can provide critical information about its development, which then gives us the opportunity to find its hidden weaknesses and vulnerabilities. With this information, we can then fashion specific corrective procedures to target and exploit those weaknesses.

1. Inclinations and reflexes you are *born* with (instincts). These are actions and automatic tendencies that you did not have to learn or be taught.

2. Things you *discover* on your own about behaviors you can do (mimic learning). These are the actions you observe in other people, discover you can do yourself, and then decide to mimic.

3. Habits and behavioral styles you unintentionally *absorb* from other people you are frequently around (passive learning). These are the predictable behaviors that you picked up from other people without realizing it.

4. Actions and behaviors which you are purposefully *taught* (training). These are both the attitudes and the behaviors acquired through systematic behavior-shaping enterprises such as education and training.

5. Things you think, feel and do which are *combinations* of all the above sources (synthesized learning). These attitudes and behaviors are the result of multiple origins and often contain elements from each of the previous sources.

The Germ Within

Certain forms of call reluctance are extremely contagious. Managers and sales trainers have been identified as carriers of call reluctance germs. Many unintentionally infect some of their most promising salespeople.

Most salespeople initially learn how to cope with call reluctance from their managers, sales trainers or training consultants who themselves may be silently struggling with the same problem. Data from management studies using the Call Reluctance Scale, a specialized test constructed specifically to detect the fear of self-promotion, reveals that a salesperson who has been exposed to a call reluctant sales management team tends to have toxic levels of call reluctance. But does that prove that managers pass call reluctance on to their sales force? Couldn't it just as easily be interpreted the other way? It could. But additional research produced more conclusive evidence.

Pre and post hiring studies with the same test found that new salespeople starting out with average or below average amounts of call reluctance tended to develop as much call reluctance as was found in their managers, trainers and consultants.

If these salespeople did not have call reluctance *before* their exposure to management, and then acquired it in the *same form* and to the *same degree* as their managers, where do you suppose it came from?

THE SEARCH FOR AN ANSWER

Typically, when salespeople show signs of struggling with call reluctance, some well-intentioned but misguided sales managers seek the aid of priestly exorcists from the psychological fast-food industry. A rich blend of ceremonial ritual, mysterious jargon and evangelistic zeal reassures management that the frustrations and fears of call reluctance will quickly yield to a 45-minute inspirational cassette or be soothed away by the gentle incantations of a stress manager. Due to prohibitive costs and less-than-spectacular results with cases of genuine call reluctance, most managers do not err in this direction more than once or twice. Inspirational cassettes can't coax it away. Threats can't scare it away. And if you ignore it, it won't just go away.

If Nancy, Bob and Larry are like most salespeople, their early training carried with it the implicit attitude-shaping message that prospecting is a scourge, a necessary evil inexorably associated with a career in direct sales. Their attitudes may have become even more fatalistically fixed by cynical sales managers or veteran salespeople who never learned how to overcome the problem themselves. Their attitude is simply that call reluctance "comes with the territory."

Veteran salespeople will recall that a few years ago sales training programs were porous, brittle structures welded together by reckless speculation and ancient folklore. Actual research was the exception. When consultants claimed to have "researched" the topic, they really meant that they had an *interest* in the subject or that they had *read* about it somewhere. There was very little systematic research conducted over the years on the subject of call reluctance. Fortunately, however, many of the time-worn sales training practices and the superficial stereotypes on which they were based have now been edged out by bold new technologies like psychologist Ed Timmons' *Sales Dynamics* and Wilson Learning's *Counselor Selling*. Both of these programs represent significant milestones because they marked the end of folkloric sales training and heralded the advent of modern behavioral science technology within the sales training field.

Progress in sales training continues. Since 1970, a small dedicated group of serious researchers have been attacking call reluctance head-on. The sound of the collision, like that from the two milestone programs mentioned above, is being heard throughout the sales training profession. The result is that in many organizations, call reluctance is finally being prevented from occurring in many salespeople, and is being corrected when it does occur in others.

THE PROSPECTING EKG

Proper intervention starts with proper assessment. Sophisticated tests and rating scales exist for that purpose. Sales training organizations will find the added diagnostic precision provided by them to be invaluable. Though not as precise, the following two procedures are provided to help you get started. They are sufficient to help determine your present call reluctance profile.

The following questions have two purposes. First, like an EKG, your answers provide an indication of how your prospecting heart is functioning at the present time. Second, you will learn which *particular* type(s) of call reluctance you may be most susceptible to. So take out a piece of paper and answer each of the following questions as honestly as you can.

1. How many contacts did you initiate with prospective clients during your last full work week?

2. Approximately how much time do you invest in preparation for each new prospecting contact you make?

3. How many group or seminar selling presentations did you schedule during the last month?

4. How many sales conversations did you initiate with your personal friends and acquaintances during the last month?

5. How many sales-related conversations did you initiate with people while attending civic, social, fraternal, political or religious meetings during the last month?

6. How many prospecting appointments or sales interviews did you have to reschedule during the last month?

7. How many sales contacts or conversations did you try to initiate last week with professional persons or wealthy, influential community leaders?

8. How many sales-related conversations did you initiate during the last three months with members of your own family? (Skip this question if you do not live in an area where you can visit members of your family with reasonable frequency.)

9. Describe any circumstances which you believe had a significant influence on how you answered the above questions. Also, if you wish, you may include comments about the questions themselves.

Analyzing Your EKG

What is "normal?" That depends. Prospecting varies from industry to industry, company to company within the same industry, and even among local branches of the same company. So acceptable prospecting activity in one sales setting could be a serious problem in another. We suggest you solicit the help of your sales manager or trainer. He or she will bring another perspective to your answers and possibly help you better understand whether they are high, low or average for *your* sales organization. (The call reluctance types will be explained in detail in Chapter Three.)

Question 1: A significantly lower-than-average number could indicate the presence of *threat sensitive* call reluctance.

Question 2: A significantly larger-than-average block of time could indicate the presence of *desurgent* call reluctance.

Question 3: A much lower-than-average number could indicate the presence of *group* call reluctance.

Question 4: A figure well below what is *possible* for you may indicate reluctance to call on your personal *friends*.

Question 5: A number significantly less than the opportunities available to you could indicate *role acceptance* call reluctance.

Question 6: A larger-than-average number could indicate the presence of *disruption sensitivity* call reluctance.

Question 7: A lower-than-average number, or a number lower than the opportunities available to you, could indicate the presence of *social differential* call reluctance.

Question 8: If you *could* have made significantly more contacts than you *did*, you could be reluctant to call on members of your own *family*.

Question 9: If you wrote or even thought of a lot of critical comments (especially *in regards to the questions themselves or how they were asked*), or if you listed *several excuses* for not making as many contacts as you could or should have, then you could have *protensive* call reluctance.

Call Reluctance Self-Rating Scale

Before drawing any final conclusions, let's take a second picture from another angle. Take a few minutes to answer each of the following questions as honestly as you can. Each requires a simple yes or no response. Write your answers on a separate piece of paper.

1. I probably spend more time planning to promote myself than I spend actually *doing* it. Yes or no?

2. I'm probably not really trying to promote myself, or my products or services, as much as I could or should because I'm not sure it's worth the hassle any more. Yes or no?

3. I probably don't try as much as I could or should to initiate contact with influential people in my community who could be prospects for my products or services. Yes or no?

4. I tend to get really uncomfortable when I have to call someone on the telephone who I don't know, and who is not expecting the call, to ask them to do something they may not want to do. Yes or no?

5. Personally, I think that having to call people who I don't know, and who are not expecting my call, to promote myself or my products/services is demeaning. Yes or no?

6. Personally, self-promotion doesn't really bother me. I just don't apply myself to it very purposefully or consistently. Yes or no?

7. I would avoid giving a presentation to a group if I could. Yes or no?

8. Actually, prospecting doesn't really bother me. I could initiate more contacts if I were not involved in so many other activities. Yes or no?

9. I have clear goals and I like to talk about them; actually, I probably spend more time talking about them than working towards them. Yes or no?

10. I seem to need some time to "psych myself up" before I can prospect. Yes or no?

11. I tend to spend a lot of time shuffling, planning, prioritizing and organizing the names on my prospecting list (or cards) before I actually put them to use. Yes or no?

12. Making cold calls (calling on people I don't know, who are not expecting me, and who may not want to talk with me) would really be difficult for me. Yes or no?

13. I tend to feel somewhat uneasy when I self-promote because deep down I probably think that promoting yourself is not really respectable or proper. Yes or no?

14. To me, making sales presentations to my friends is unacceptable because it would look like I was trying to exploit their friendship. Yes or no?

15. I often feel like I am intruding on people when I prospect. Yes or no?

16. To me, making sales presentations to members of my own family is out of bounds because it might look like I was trying to exploit my own relatives. Yes or no?

17. It is very important to me to find innovative, alternative ways to prospect and self-promote which are more dignified than the methods used by other salespeople. Yes or no?

18. I think that prospecting probably takes more out of me emotionally than other salespeople. Yes or no?

19. I would probably do all right one-on-one, but I would get pretty nervous if I found out that I had to give a sales presentation to a large group of people. Yes or no?

20. Highly educated, professional people like lawyers and doctors tend to annoy me, so I don't *try* to initiate promotional contact with them even though I probably could if I wanted to. Yes or no?

Scoring your Call Reluctance Self-Rating Scale

There are two steps to evaluating the Call Reluctance Self-Rating Scale. Both are quick and easy.

Step One:

Compute your overall call reluctance score by adding up your "yes" responses. Then read the following interpretive summary which is based on your total number of "yes" answers.

Total Number "Yes" Answers	Interpretation
1-2	Indicates one of two conditions: Either you are experiencing no emotional difficulty associated with prospecting (self-promotion) at the present time, or you are experiencing distress but are hesitant to reveal how much.
3-4	Indicates that you are like most other salespeople. The fear of self-promotion is present, but only in low, non-toxic amounts. It may be occasionally annoying, but it is not likely to be serious if it remains at this level. It should be manageable by simply emphasizing the markets and prospecting techniques you are most comfortable with and avoiding those which are the most tender. This book, however, is still recommended, not because it is critically necessary now, but because it can strengthen your tender prospecting areas, and by so doing, open up even more prospecting possibilities.
5-6	You could have moderate levels of call reluctance at the present time. One or more forms of the fear of self-promotion are currently limiting your prospecting to a level below your ability. Your prospecting is probably out of sync with your market potential. The remaining sections of this book should be personally and financially rewarding.
7-8	Your answers indicate a considerable amount of call reluctance at the present time. Your prospecting is probably only a shadow of what it could or needs to be. But don't despair. Instead, fasten your seat belt and get ready for some serious self-confrontation.
9 or more	Do you glow in the dark? You could have enough call reluctance to stop a small sales force. Do you make *any* sales calls? Your attitudes about prospecting suggest that you must be working for a manager who has the patience of a saint, a company with no performance standards, or you're a self-employed consultant.

If your answers are truly indicative of your attitudes towards prospecting and self-promotion, then you should consider taking immediate corrective steps. Honestly discuss the problem with your manager or sales trainer if he or she does not already know about it. That's important. Then continue reading. Be certain to follow the instructions carefully for each of the procedures. This book can help you turn your career around if you will let it.

One other interpretation is possible. You may be too self-critical. When you took Abnormal Psychology class, you were certain you had *every one* of the pathologies you learned about. In church, you are certain your clergyman is looking accusingly at *you*. When completing any test or rating scale, such as this one, you believe that the most self-critical statements always apply to you. If you think you have been too hard on yourself, lighten up and go through the scale once again.

Does your score indicate that call reluctance could be limiting your performance? If it does, look at step two. It will help you pinpoint the specific *type(s)* of call reluctance which may have arrested your prospecting ability and imprisoned your sales career.

Step Two:

Call reluctance doesn't just happen. Like a virus, it has a developmental history, comes in a variety of flavors, and leaves clues in the form of attitudinal footprints along the way. Use the following chart to review each of your "yes" answers on the Call Reluctance Self-Rating Scale. It will help you determine which particular *type(s)* of call reluctance you might currently have, or which strains you might be most susceptible to in the future. For the present, don't worry about what each type of call reluctance or impostor means. The impostors will be covered in Chapter Two. The nine types of call reluctance will be covered in detail in Chapter Three.

Question Number	Type of Call Reluctance or Impostor	Question Number	Type of Call Reluctance or Impostor
1, 11	Desurgency	8	Impostor (Goal Diffusion)
2	Impostor (Low Goals)	9	Impostor (Goals Misaligned)
3, 20	Social Differential	10, 13	Role Acceptance
4, 12, 18	Threat Sensitivity	14	Friends
5, 17	Protension	15	Disruption Sensitivity
6	Impostor (Low Motivation)	16	Family
7, 19	Groups		

Final Word

The Prospecting EKG and the Call Reluctance Self-Rating Scale have given you an opportunity to review your orientation towards prospecting and self-promotion. Together, they work like a flawed but valuable mirror. They reflect your prospecting image. When you hold up the mirror and look squarely into it, what do you see? Are you looking at the face of call reluctance?

Low prospecting activity means you <u>could</u> have call reluctance. But it does not mean you <u>do</u>. Three essential conditions—motivation, goals and goal-obstructing feelings— must be present before you can conclude that you have authentic call reluctance.

CHAPTER TWO

THE CALL RELUCTANCE IMPOSTORS

IT LOOKS LIKE CALL RELUCTANCE, BUT IS IT?

Sales managers often come to the Call Reluctance Center when they are confronted with low prospecting activity and their own training resources break down. Billy was a good example. "He's broke. Fix him!" ordered Billy, the harsh looking, but amiable, real estate trainer who always had a cigar poking out from his face and spoke out of the side of his mouth. "He used to be a heavy hitter, but now he won't prospect. Got call reluctance," he continued, emphasizing each syllable and making it sound as important as an entire sentence. Billy had just paid a well-known psychologist to conduct a group session for his entire agency. The psychologist had carp-like lips, spoke with a lisp, and drooled as he ordered the agents to stretch out on the training room floor and relax. It didn't work. The entire sales force rolled on the floor and laughed to the point of pain every time the psychologist spoke. Each time he exhorted them to let their minds wander and relax, they laughed even more. Billy was not amused.

After two hours at the Call Reluctance Center, Billy's agent had completed the Call Reluctance Scale and the Sales Profile Analysis. From his test results, it was clear that he had a problem, but it was not call reluctance. On the surface it looked like call reluctance, but it would not respond to the call reluctance treatments. What was it?

Although call reluctance usually plays an important role in prospecting problems, there are notable exceptions. They're called "impostors." Only by knowing what they are and how they work, can you be sure that it's call reluctance which is limiting your self-promotional efforts and not an impostor. But to do that, you must first understand exactly what call reluctance is.

PRODUCT DEFINITION:
What Call Reluctance Does to Prospecting Activity

Most presentations on call reluctance surge right past the smoldering issue of how it is defined. The practice of ceremoniously calling it a *name*, like the "fear of failure," and then moving on to other matters is probably the main reason for the continued confusion and lack of progress in this area.

Perhaps the most compelling evidence of call reluctance in salespeople comes from its effect on prospecting activity. **Prospecting activity is the total number of face-to-face and telephone contacts initiated with prospective clients.**

Genuine call reluctance always results in low prospecting activity. But what is low activity? Low is a relative term. Its definition differs among individuals and organizations. **Low activity is always defined as insufficient prospecting to sustain personal or corporate performance objectives.** That means not enough contacts are being initiated with prospective buyers to support your own career objectives or your organization's performance requirements. Either one spells trouble.

PROCESS DEFINITION:
Conditions Necessary for Call Reluctance to Occur

A fever *could* mean you have the flu. It could also mean something else. Low prospecting activity means you *could* have call reluctance. But it does not mean you *do*. **Three essential conditions —motivation, goals and goal-obstructing feelings— must be present before you can conclude that you have authentic call reluctance.** If prospecting activity is low and one of these conditions is missing, you're a call reluctance impostor. It is very important to be able to tell one from the other. The process definition provides an organized and systematic guide to evaluating call reluctance.

An electrician's schematic diagram allows the skilled technician to compare the measured values he observes at key points against the values his diagram indicates should be there. If one of these values is missing or incorrect, the electrician knows he has a problem and exactly which circuit is responsible. Armed with that information, he can fix the problem.

The process definition of call reluctance involves taking measurements from three separate points. These measurements indicate the status of critical mental circuits which influence your prospecting activity. To conclude that your low prospecting activity is due to genuine call reluctance, measurements must first be taken of your motivation, goals, and goal-obstructing feelings.

Motivation

Motivation is an "in" word. Everybody uses it, and it seems that everybody has their own definition. But what does motivation mean to *you*? How do you use it? Whatever it is, you can't have authentic call reluctance without it.

Who Cares?

Some salespeople and their managers think that highly emotional training problems such as anger, depression and volatile forms of call reluctance are deadly. We agree that they're never fun and must always be taken seriously. But they're not the most deadly problem faced by sales trainers. That distinction is reserved for a situation which is far more difficult and perhaps even impossible to deal with, low motivation. It can surface in one of three disconcerting, energy-robbing behavioral addictions: lethargy, disinterest or apathy. Either one is a career killer.

Salespeople who secretly don't *care* about better performance are unreachable. In response, many sales managers and trainers attempt to cope with the situation by doing their "wanting" for them. But that never works. *You* have to be *self*-energized. *You have to do your own wanting.* That's one thing you must bring *with you* to any career.

To the unmotivated, there are never urgent performance problems, and unexpected opportunities never beckon. These things exist only in the minds of managers and trainers. Performance limiting problems, however, such as anger, depression and call reluctance, are different. They are the outward emotional signs of intense, but conflicting, internal wanting. You cannot experience them unless you first *want* something deeply. As performance problems go, they are perplexing but they also *have a positive side*. They indicate the presence of a rich layer of motivational energy which can be tapped to help solve the problem and improve performance.

Apathy, lethargy and disinterest darken the outlook. They provide insufficient fuel for enlightenment or improvement. Salespeople with these conditions don't *want* to improve. Outside of prayer, they don't give sales trainers anything significant to work with. Do you really care about your sales career? How much?

Three facets of motivation can be measured: amplitude, duration and velocity. To assess motivation, most modern sales organizations supplement their informal assessment procedures, such as interviewing and personal observation, with formal testing instruments like Athena*Tech and the Motivation Analysis Test. Though not absolutely necessary, they can add a valuable objective dimension to the measurement of the following three aspects of motivation.

Amplitude

This is a measure of the power in the circuit. It tells us how *much* you want to prospect. Amplitude is the measurement of motivational energy like the 110 volts you need in your wall plug to make your television work. If it is not there, or if it is present but less than 110 volts, your television won't work. But is it the fault of your television? No. The problem is insufficient power to meet the needs of the application. Some companies try to wire in 50 volt salespeople to 110 volt sales careers. Under such conditions, prospecting will not be sufficient. But is it due to call reluctance? No, that's a logical impossibility. How can you be considered *reluctant* when you are not doing *what you don't want to do in the first place*?

Duration

In order for your television to work, it must have 110 volts *constantly*. It can't have 110 volts for a week and then take a two week vacation. So we are interested in trying to estimate how *long* the level of available motivation lasts. Some salespeople need to reach a minimal level of performance. Once that *need* is met, they slack off until it arises again. Naturally, during "down" time, prospecting is not going to be at peak levels. In such cases, when prospecting drops off, it is due to declining *desire*, not emotional hesitation.

Velocity

Events don't always occur at the same speed. Some salespeople are high octane individuals who translate their motivation into behavior at a fast and intense rate. Others are more laid back and serene. This is the result of a stylistic difference among salespeople and is more useful for predicting other performance problems such as low frustration tolerance and burnout. Although helpful, in most cases this measurement is not needed to deal with call reluctance.

Are you motivated? Do you have enough *want* to prospect? To prospect successfully, motivation is necessary, but it is not *sufficient* in and of itself. There are plenty of motivated salespeople who are not call reluctant but who are nevertheless stuck at marginal levels of prospecting performance. That brings us to the second critical measurement point, goals.

Goals

Motivation is energy. In order to work, it needs to be connected *to* something. For a television to work, it must first be plugged into a wall socket. Only then can the electrical energy be discharged through the wires to the set where it energizes the circuits necessary to produce sound and pictures. Goal assessment is the process of evaluating what your motivation is connected to. In the case of call reluctance, it's very important. Here's what you should look for.

Target   This is *what* you want. It provides the meaning behind your prospecting efforts. Where do your motivational wires lead? What is your motivation connected to? Ideally, you should have clearly focused career goals to support your prospecting activities. And these goals should be *accomplishable where you are*, not somewhere else. If they are not, your motivation will be disconnected from any *available* goals. Motivation without firm, supportive goals becomes a mindless struggle without meaning. Eventually, your drive overpowers your direction. Prospecting becomes mechanistic and tedious, boring you to sleep behind the wheel of your career. Prospecting activity then drops off. But is it due to call reluctance? No. It is due to disinterest, not fear.

Strategy   Some salespeople take pride in being able to *recite* their goals and ambitions at the drop of a hat. It impresses people. It probably helped them get their current sales position. But if you poke beneath the cloud cover, you don't find much else. No thought. No purpose. No planning. Just recitation for effect. Without a plan for reaching their goals, they easily get sidetracked or just plain lost. One of the first performance areas to suffer the consequences is prospecting. But salespeople who don't plan their prospecting consistently are not call reluctant. They're *confused*.

Pursuit

Some salespeople target their goals and then spend endless hours constructing elaborate lists, plans and strategies for reaching them. The trouble is, *they don't do anything else*. They don't devote much motivational energy to actually carrying out their plans. There's no target pursuit. Are they call reluctant? No. They would simply rather talk and plan than prospect and promote.

Are You a Driver or a Striver?

During the 1970's, it became fashionable in some circles to insist that good salespeople had to be *drivers*. The term driver was used to describe salespeople before that time, but by the 70's it had become a part of our vocabulary. But experience has not been kind to drivers. The concept has not aged well. Why? Because drivers did not live up to their billing. They were valued for their motion; nobody bothered to check their sense of direction. The result was a group of forceful salespeople who were unable or unwilling to see or plan ahead, one of the basic elements behind any *long*-term career choice. Consequently, to the disappointment of managers, trainers and colleagues alike, their commitment to any given sales organization was *not* long-term. Their tenure was dismal.

Since that time, other studies based on more sophisticated and universally accepted personality tests have found that drivers need a steering wheel to match their engine size. We call that combination a *striver*, a driver with a *goal*.

Goal-Disrupting Feelings

The third condition completes the triangle of influences necessary for authentic call reluctance to be present. A motivated, goal-directed salesperson must be tripping over self-imposed mental obstacles as he tries to translate his motivation into goal-reaching behaviors.

Let's return to the television analogy. First, we plug the television into an energy supply in the wall. If all is well, the energy flows from the wall through the wires to the set where it enables the set to perform. But what if there is a short circuit along the way? Some or all of the energy is *diverted* at the short circuit and never gets to the set. No picture. No sound. **Call reluctance is an emotional short circuit in an energized, goal-directed salesperson**. The energy destined for prospecting gets short circuited into coping. Instead of being used to enable prospecting, it's depleted by wishing, waiting, whining, blaming and pouting.

THE FOUR GREAT IMPOSTORS

When either motivation, goals or goal-disrupting feelings are missing, you undoubtedly still have a prospecting problem, but it is not due to call reluctance. *It's an impostor.*

Impostors have several important features. First, they always lack one or more of the three essential conditions reviewed above. Second, they are accompanied by low prospecting activity that mimics the product definition of authentic call reluctance (which is why both a product and a process definition are needed). Third, they don't respond to treatments designed to correct authentic call reluctance.

Are you prospecting below your ability? Are you call reluctant or are you an impostor? It's important to find out. Let's look at each of the impostors in more detail.

Low Motivation, High Goals
"All talk, no action"

$$m \rightarrow G$$

Some salespeople just aren't motivated at all. Some are not motivated *enough* to succeed in direct sales. What about you? If you are not prospecting because you don't *want* to, then you don't have call *reluctance*. You can't. You have low motivation. The result, low activity, may be the same as call reluctance, but there the similarity ends.

Daryl, a headhunter for a large national firm, was not prospecting enough to satisfy Blair, his manager. Since he recited clear-cut goals, Blair immediately assumed he had call reluctance and sent him to the Call Reluctance Center. The Sales Profile Analysis (SPA) was the first of a series of tests Daryl completed, but it was all we needed. Daryl was an impostor. Below is part of the summary report from his SPA.

Prospecting . . . . Low

Closing . . . . Very Low

Learning . . . . Low

Self-Directed Career Management . . . . Low

Durability . . . . Low

Motivated salespeople balance weaknesses against strengths. But Daryl didn't want to prospect, or close, or learn new products, or take responsibility for his own career, or tolerate any frustrations. Daryl was an impostor. He couldn't be considered reluctant to go after what he didn't want.

High Motivation, Too Many Goals
Goal diffusion

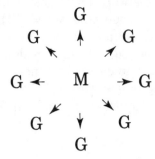

Some salespeople are adrift in their own possibilities. Seeing life as an adventure and commitments as a bore, they become *addicted* to the celebration of their own freedom. Alan, a bright and exuberant young manufacturer's rep, bounced from subject to subject whenever he spoke. He was, to use his own decorous words, "a Renaissance man." He prided himself on his many interests, relationships and involvements. When he was evaluated by his company's new sales assessment center, the observers were enchanted by his broad interests and keen intellect. Noting this, and also his congenial social skills, the assessors unanimously predicted high sales achievement. But once outside the simulated reality of the sales assessment center, Alan's work habits became the subject of immediate critical concern. He showed up for prospecting training late or not at all. When asked for an explanation from management, he didn't seem to grasp that there *was* a problem. If there indeed was a problem, it was not *his*. He was content. His habitual reaction to any criticism was a smiling disbelief. "Why is everyone so *materialistic* all the time, anyway?" he repeatedly asked himself.

One day Alan was called at home by his training manager because he was late for a scheduled sales training session.

MGR: Hi, Alan, I thought we had agreed to begin your training last night at 7 p.m. We were here waiting. Where were you?

ALAN: Gosh, I'm sorry guys. I guess I just plain missed it, didn't I? I went on down to the wine and cheese tasting party at the Fairmont with my girlfriend.

MGR: *Wine and cheese tasting party? You missed the prospecting training program for a wine and cheese tasting party?*

ALAN: Yeah, I guess so. But it won't happen again. Sorry.

MGR: Okay. Let's see that it doesn't.

Two evenings later:

MGR: Alan? Where were you *last* night? I thought you said you would be here on Tuesday evenings for telephone prospecting. What happened this time?

ALAN: Golly, I'm sorry. Guess I'm just not organized enough. I forgot to tell you I have lute lessons every Tuesday evening. Great stuff. You should try it. . .

MGR: *Lute lessons?* Well, how about nine in the morning?

ALAN: That would be great. Oh, wait a minute. I don't think I can make that.

MGR: Oh? Why not?

ALAN: Well, a group of us registered for a medieval metaphysical poetry course at the junior college. It meets every Wednesday morning at nine. A friend of mine said it changed her life. Want to sign up with us?

Alan is motivated. He's a high energy person, but his energy is not *usable* because it is not focused on anything specific. There's no target. No strategy. No systematic pursuit. His prospecting will never get off the ground because it can't compete with "other interesting things to do." But Alan will never be accomplished in any of them. Instead, he will remain inert, starting much completing little, interested in everything mastering nothing. Alan's not call reluctant. He's an impostor.

High Motivation, No Goals
"All dressed up, no place to go"

$$M \rightarrow g$$

Some salespeople are fully charged with energy, but don't have a clue about what to do with it. So instead of finding meaning for their lives and careers, they borrow what seems to be working for other sales-people and mindlessly dump their motivation into it. It could be recognition which comes from being top producer, approval of one's parents, or money which comes from high production. These are worthwhile goals, but if they're not *your* goals, the pressures of prospecting and selling will eventually consume them. When that happens, they will be unable to provide you with direction. Performance problems that are not related to call reluctance, such as burnout and midlife crisis, will rip the rug right out from under you. Prospecting levels will drop to dangerous lows. It will look and feel like call reluctance, but it won't be. It's an impostor. The engine outruns the steering wheel and mindlessly follows other cars down the freeway at break-neck speed until it runs out of gas. You can suspect this impostor when you can no longer easily answer the question, "What am I prospecting *for?*"

No one becomes lazy except in the pursuit of someone else's goals.

High Motivation, High Goals, Low Training
"I'll prospect when I know what to say"

$$M \rightarrow G \rightarrow ?$$

Some motivated, goal-directed salespeople hesitate to initiate contacts with prospective buyers because they feel they have not yet been adequately trained to ethically represent their products and services to the community. This happens when high quality salespeople are hired into low quality sales organizations. For our purposes, we do not distinguish organizational quality by the the type of product or service sold, but rather by the quality of sales *management* and depth of preparation and training they provide.

In low quality sales organizations, careers are designed to be short-term infatuations. The prevailing attitude towards sales training does not provide for the long haul. These organizations don't expect a salesperson to stay, and they don't particularly care when he leaves. What's important to them is that the salesperson generates big profits while there.

Training is rarely formal or systematic. Instead, the process begins with "Sign here." It ends with a slap on the back, a shove out the door, and a heartfelt, "Sick 'em tiger!" High quality salespeople expect more. They also need more before they can allow themselves to feel good about the products or services they sell. Their refusal to initiate contact with prospective buyers is an act of intellect and integrity. It is not an act of fear. It is not call reluctance. They're information impostors.

If you are an information impostor, then your hesitation to prospect can be cleared up quickly and easily by the information you need. Just ask for it from your sales manager or trainer. That should do the trick. But there's a catch. After you have received the additional information you said you needed, you should be ready to make more calls, immediately. If on the other hand, you still need more information before you can make calls, then ask for it, too. Ask as often as you need. *Now* are you ready to make your calls?

If your prospecting activity is low because you are an information impostor, you will be "cured" by the information you say you need. The problem will be corrected *by the information.* Improved prospecting activity should immediately follow. But if you still find yourself asking for *more* information, then it's obvious *that information was never the problem in the first place.* It was an *excuse.* You have one of the nine authentic forms of call reluctance. It's called Desurgency. Desurgency and the other eight types of authentic call reluctance are described in the next chapter.

GAMES IMPOSTORS PLAY

Impostors tend to be comfortable with familiar habits of living and coping. They know they are not performing at or even near their potential. But since any treatment always contains an element of risk and uncertainty, impostors cope by rigorously *avoiding* the solutions they need the most. They turn to less threatening techniques. Often, their avoidance is so complete and predictable that you can infer what they need by observing what they *avoid.*

Goal-Setting Junkies

Impostors who recite goals but lack the motivation to reach them, know they have a problem. But they seek their medicine among their poison. They sign up for every goal-setting conference, seminar and workshop they can get to. They extend their vocabulary and learn concepts and procedures which would be useful if in fact goal-setting was their problem. It's not, but it's something they are comfortable with. They know a lot about it. It's not threatening. Notice, however, what they dutifully avoid, *motivational* workshops. They resist that which could help them the most. Paradoxically, the result is career anemia. They eat a lot, but all the wrong foods.

Inspirational Junkies

Impostors who need to establish order in their lives and careers attend every motivational workshop they can. When they are not marching off to workshops, they are listening to inspirational cassettes. They drown themselves in platitudes and dream in motivational slogans. But they consistently avoid what they need, *goal-setting*.

Time Management Junkies

Impostors who lack the ability to clarify and sort out what is most important in their lives, know they have an energy allocation problem. They find themselves scattered in every direction and lost among their multiple needs, desires and interests. They never learned how to differentiate what they would *like* from what they actually *need*. Weighted down by chaos and fragmentation, they look to books on planning and time management for *all* their answers. None of these solutions stick. So they keep looking. Avoiding their real need for values clarification, they remain lost in a maze of planning techniques and time management procedures.

REMEDIES AND POISONS

Impostor	Time Mgt.	Values Clarif.	Goal Setng.	Product Trng.	Motivation Training
			Remedies		
Low Mot.	NE	NE	P	NE	B
No Goals	NE	NE	B	P	NE
Goal Diffusion	NE	B	B	NE	P
Information	P	P	P	B	P

Key: NE= Not harmful or helpful. Probably not effective.
     B= Probably beneficial.
     P= Poisonous. Can make matters worse.

The impostors are as lethal to a career in direct sales as authentic call reluctance. They mimic the low production associated with the real thing. But they are missing one or more of the three essential conditions necessary for genuine call reluctance, and they don't respond well to the procedures designed to correct it.

The first thing a salesperson, manager, trainer or consultant should do before treating call reluctance is to rule out the impostors.

But beware. Most pop-psych approaches to evaluating call reluctance fall woefully short. For example, typical selection tests are unable to distinguish authentic call reluctance from other causes of low prospecting activity. Even good tests in the wrong hands can produce misleading results. We recommend only specialized testing and evaluation procedures which may be available through your company's sales training or personnel department.

Recalculating Losses

Once call reluctance is properly defined, its epidemic impact can be more clearly observed and understood. We now know, for example, that up to 40% of all salespeople who are said to fail each year due to call reluctance are actually impostors. In many cases, they are casualties of rigid but superficial sales selection programs which led to grossly inaccurate hiring decisions. In other cases, they are the victims of unintentional neglect due to insensitive assessment procedures which result in the wrong training weapons being aimed at the wrong training targets.

Recommendations for Impostors

This book is dedicated to the correction of authentic call reluctance. It could not be kept to a readable size if we included corrective methods for impostors. Perhaps that volume will come later. If you determine that you are an impostor, you should talk to your manager or trainer, or try to seek out corrective information and resources on your own. We have provided some initial guidance to help you get started in the right direction. Although this short list is far from complete, it is representative of the kinds of worthwhile advice which is currently available.

Seeds of Greatness, by Dennis Waitley, Pocket Books, 1983.

A Christmas Carol, by Charles Dickens, James H. Heineman, 1967.

What Color Is Your Parachute? by Richard Bolles, Ten Speed Press, 1978.

The Three Boxes Of Life, by Richard Bolles, Ten Speed Press, 1978.

Debunking a Call Reluctance Myth

Back in sales training antiquity (ten years ago), we happened to be present to hear a weather-beaten, crusty old sales manager, who we'll call Buford, speak at his industry's annual sales management convention. A young protégé in the audience stood and asked him to comment on call reluctance. Buford affected a weariness that he didn't really feel and theatrically closed his eyes for a long moment like he was privately receiving the answer straight from heaven. "Call reluctance?" he said slowly, stretching each syllable, "You want to know about call reluctance? I'll tell you about call reluctance. Show me a call reluctant salesman (*they were all men back then*) and I'll show you a lazy SOB who doesn't believe in our product." Wheezing and fuming, Buford went on, "He ain't got no commitment. That's all you need to know about call reluctance." With that, Buford verbally wiped call reluctance from the board like an incorrect answer to a elementary math problem. But he spoke the truth as it was known back then. He held the majority opinion. But times have changed. We now know differently.

The process definition of call reluctance firmly establishes that no salesperson (male or female) can be call reluctant unless they are both motivated and committed. You simply cannot be reluctant to get something you don't want in the first place. Impostors don't care if they don't meet their prospecting goals. Salespeople with authentic call reluctance care *very much*. Imagine the pain and energy required to continuously try to prospect day-after-day regardless of constant distress. What keeps these salespeople going if not motivation and commitment? It's certainly not job satisfaction! Salespeople with authentic call reluctance hang in as long as they can, usually until the system expels them. Impostors leave soon after their first confrontation with sales management.

Paradoxically, sales managers have tried for years to attract motivated and committed salespeople. Ironically, many have always been around. They just happened to be *imperfect*; they had call reluctance. But thanks in part to great social scientists like Buford, call reluctance was considered to be a character flaw, an absence of willpower, or a lack of commitment to the company or product. The ready solution was to get the heretic ". . .right the hell out of the business!"

Companies did. Motivated salespeople who happened to have call reluctance were either branded with a scarlet letter or neglected altogether. It cost both the companies and the salespeople dearly. In some companies and industries it still does.

In addition, many specialized training courses are available for salespeople and sales managers. Some of the best that we're familiar with are offered by the following:

The Corporate Educator, Garland, Texas
(Time management and goal-setting courses)

Dr. Edwin O. Timmons, Baton Rouge, Louisiana
(*Sales Dynamics* and *Behavioral Dynamics* training courses)

Wilson Learning Corporation, Minneapolis, Minnesota
(*Counselor Selling training course*)

Dennis Waitley, Inc., Ranch Springs, Sante Fe, California

How to Evaluate Call Reluctance "Experts"

The wrong information, or even the right information in the wrong hands, can make prospecting problems much worse. You can evaluate the expertise in prospective consultants and speakers by asking certain key questions in advance. Can they properly *define* call reluctance? Do they use *both* the process and the product definitions? Do they account for the three essential conditions? And most important, *do they recognize the impostors*? If they don't, fasten your seat belt and hold on to your wallet. You are about to be taken on an expensive and wasteful ride.

The notion that call reluctance is a single condition is a venerable piece of nonsense which has largely been discredited. Nine different types have been identified so far and there are probably more.

CHAPTER THREE
THE NINE FACES
OF CALL RELUCTANCE

CONFRONTING THE ENEMY

Like many before us, we launched our research in 1970 under the assumption that we were embarking on an exploration to locate and observe a single performance-limiting condition. But the popular understanding, that call reluctance could be neatly shrunk down to one or two simplistic notions like the "fear of rejection" or the "fear of failure," soon withered and died under the strain of mounting evidence. Nine different types have been identified so far. There are probably more. We are still searching.

The notion that call reluctance is a single condition is a venerable piece of nonsense which has largely been discredited. The territory inhabited by the fear of self-promotion is a bittersweet, colorful but hostile land where motivated, goal-directed ambitions rub elbows with energy-robbing attitudes.

Let's return to Nancy, Bob and Larry, the three actual case examples we used to introduce Chapter One. Nancy is fighting a form of authentic call reluctance called Threat Sensitivity. It is characterized by a paralyz-

---

Definition of a Sales Professional

One question is asked more frequently than any other when we speak at sales conventions. It is, "What is your definition of a sales professional?" There are many answers to that question. We're not sure our definition is better than any other. But from the perspective of our work with the fear of self-promotion, one definition does emerge:

A truly professional salesperson is an individual who has the ability and the emotional discipline necessary to make cold calls when they are necessary, but who has been trained so well that he never has to.

ing, self-protective, over-precautionary vigilance. Threat sensitive people, like Nancy, tend to presume that things are bound to go wrong. They divert too much of their motivational energy to being prepared for the worst. They are perpetually on "red alert." To them, any risk-taking is distressful. Since initiating contact with prospective buyers requires taking a social risk, it becomes difficult, if not impossible, for them to do so without corrective training.

Bob limits himself by refusing to call on any of his friends or relatives. He has both family and friends call reluctance. Typically, someone like Bob fashions elaborate, sometimes belligerent, ethical arguments to excuse their call reluctance. "Professional salespeople," they are fond of sermonizing, "should never resort to using their own family or friends as prospects." Some get quite *emotional* when they are pressed to produce *logical* justification for their refusal to utilize the contacts closest to them. That's the key. It becomes apparent in such heated discussions that Bob's hesitation is not the result of an intellectual *choice*. It's the result of an emotional inability. *It's call reluctance.*

Variations on a Call Reluctance Theme

The fear of self-promotion is the *generic* name given to the general inhibition to promote yourself. It can limit the career progress of anyone. When it limits the ability of salespeople to prospect, it gets the name *call reluctance*. When it interferes with the ability of sales managers to contact and consistently work high quality recruitment referral sources, it is called *recruiting reluctance*. When it impedes the ability of salespeople to close sales once contact has been initiated and a presentation has been given, it is called *close reluctance*.

Both recruiting reluctance and close reluctance are blood relatives to call reluctance. But they have some important distinctions. The measurement technologies mentioned in this book can also be used to assess both of these career-limiting conditions. The corrective procedures we have provided can also be used, but may require some adjustments.

Larry doesn't have "the fear of rejection." And he doesn't *just* have call reluctance. He has *social differential call reluctance*. Social differential call reluctance is an *emotional* condition which causes salespeople to feel inferior to prospects they perceive to be socially or economically better off than they are. Larry is intimidated by wealth, education and status. He copes by aiming his prospecting efforts *downward*. He maintains prospecting comfort by sacrificing the most lucrative market for his product. By so doing, however, he defaults on his own performance goals. It's a bitter trade-off. Social differential call reluctance is particularly lethal when it occurs in salespeople with companies that sell to an up-market clientele. Without the proper training support, these salespeople can't emotionally make the grade.

Terms and Concepts

Following are some terms and concepts you should know before reviewing the nine types of call reluctance in detail.

Term or Concept	Meaning
Origin	Where a self-limiting behavior comes from; divided between heredity and learning.
Outlook	Likelihood of improvement for each call reluctance type, assuming accurate assessment and appropriate corrective procedures are used.
CareerStyle	Characteristic behavior associated with each type of call reluctance; serves as reference point for observation and diagnosis.
Self-Assessment Questions	You should ask yourself each of the questions which accompany the descriptions of the nine types of call reluctance. Answer them as honestly as you can. They may reveal that a particular type of call reluctance is limiting your career in ways you may not have previously considered.
Call Reluctance Scale	A highly specialized, formally developed questionnaire introduced in 1982. Administered by micro computer or paper-and-pencil test, it is the only test available specifically designed to measure the nine types of call reluctance.
Prospecting "Brake Score" and "Accelerator Score"	Two of the most important scores reported by the Call Reluctance Scale. Using the analogy of an automobile, the Accelerator Score is the measure

of total motivation invested in propelling the salesperson *forward* into the community to initiate contact with prospective buyers. The Brake Score is the measure of the total motivation being diverted from prospecting to *coping* behaviors (which in essence bring prospecting to a halt). Call reluctance is indicated when the Brake Score is *higher* than the Accelerator Score. Call reluctance is not present when the Brake Score is *lower* than the Accelerator Score.

Athena*Tech

Widely used micro computer-scored personality test for assessing salespeople and sales management personnel. Produces highly specialized reports which include: Call Reluctance Scale (see above), Athena*Graph (comprehensive personality report), Selling Styles Profile Analysis (see below), Compatibility Profile Analysis (measures relationship between salesperson and trainer or manager), and Sales Profile Analysis (uses cost/benefit model to forecast sales performance).

Natural Selling Style

Based on the Selling Styles Profile Analysis, part of the Athena*Tech Objective Sales Assessment System. This is a valuable training and development application of formal testing procedures which statistically graphs and provides training narrative about a salesperson's natural and secondary selling styles.

Prescriptions

Procedures found in the *Prescriptions (Rx)* section of this book designed for each type of call reluctance.

Abbreviations

The commonly accepted shorthand names for each of the nine types of call reluctance found in printouts of certain tests.

Equipped with these preliminary terms and concepts, we can now begin to explore each of the nine forms of call reluctance. Hopefully, you will identify important attitudes and behaviors which are interfering with your prospecting efforts. Identifying the type of call reluctance you are struggling with is the first and most important step to correcting it.

Overview of the Nine Types of Call Reluctance

This chart provides a brief overview of the nine types of call reluctance along with a summary of key characteristics associated with each.

Call Reluctance Type	"Marker" Behaviors
Threat Sensitivity	Will not take social risks
Desurgency	Over-analyzes, under-acts
Protension	Obsessed with image
Groups	Fears group presentations
Friends	Fears loss of friends
Role Acceptance	Ashamed of sales career
Disruption Sensitivity	Fear of intruding on others
Social Differential	Intimidated by up-market clientele
Family/Relatives	Fears loss of family approval

Threat Sensitivity

Abbreviation: TS

Capsule Summary:

Threat sensitive call reluctance occurs when salespeople become preoccupied with worst-case prospecting possibilities. They cope by staying alarmed and maintaining a high degree of emergency preparedness. This level of heightened vigilance is an emotional and physical drain on energy. It results in insufficient stamina for initiating contacts with prospective buyers on a regular basis.

Probable Origin:

Popular studies are now beginning to confirm what scholars and researchers have suspected for many years. Personality characteristics like Threat Sensitivity reflect both a *learning* and a *hereditary* parentage. This information is just now beginning to reach the popular literature. A recent newspaper article about agoraphobia, which is Threat Sensitivity out of control, announced that "Evidence is mounting that vulnerability to agoraphobia is inherited. If one identical twin has the disorder, the second twin has a 40% chance of developing it."

Outlook:

Threat Sensitivity is one of the "big three" types of call reluctance. Practically speaking, since it is a personality-based *point of view* influenced by heredity, it can be *arrested and improved upon*, but *not cured*.

CareerStyle:

- Overly alerted to low probability problems
- Appear friendly, but enjoy only limited social involvement
- Low social or emotional risk-takers
- Unrelated to intelligence, dedication or self-discipline
- Distressed by having to make cold calls either in person or on the telephone
- Highly self-controlled
- Tend to measure success by the absence of failure
- Prepare by memorizing a few scripted presentations
- Blind-sided when prospect deviates from expected scenario
- Paralyzed by spontaneity

Self-Assessment:

- How do you see prospecting in terms of social or emotional risk-taking? (Look for an imbalance of perceived danger over perceived opportunities.)
- How many total social, civic, fraternal or religious organizations are you presently *active* in? (Look for low social involvement.)
- How much do you rely on memorized sales scripts? (Look for almost exclusive reliance upon and use of scripted sales presentations.)
- How many total prospecting contacts do you initiate daily? (Look for low total number.)
- When you daydream, do you see yourself involved in reckless, devil-may-care risks and adventures? (Threat sensitive salespeople who are coping with too much self-imposed fear and restriction compensate by creating an imaginary world where they do just the opposite.)

Objective Assessments:

Call Reluctance Scale
A high prospecting Brake Score plus a high TS score indicates that

Threat Sensitivity is probably limiting prospecting performance now.

A low prospecting Brake Score plus a high TS score indicates a predisposition to threat sensitive call reluctance, although it is probably not limiting prospecting at the present time.

Selling Styles Profile Analysis
Threat sensitive salespeople tend to be need-oriented or product-oriented in their sales presentation style.

Sales Profile Analysis
Sales forecasting tests, like the Sales Profile Analysis, project threat sensitive salespeople to produce only at marginal levels due to the emotional ceiling on their prospecting.

Frequency of Occurrence:

Rare in established salespeople
Common in non-salespeople

Most Effective Treatments:

Threat Desensitization
Thought Realignment
Thought Zapping

Desurgency

Abbreviation: DSY

Capsule Summary:

Desurgent call reluctance occurs in sensitive salespeople who become anxiously concerned about being swept away by the intensity of their own feelings. To cope, they go emotionally underground, developing interests in highly technical or artistic matters. They control their feelings by keeping them under lock and out of sight. Interaction with others is conducted through emotionally safe information-bound channels. When the balance shifts too far to the information side, they tend to spend too much time preparing what to say and how to say it, while spending too little time prospecting for people to give their presentations to.

Probable Origin:

One of the "big three," desurgent call reluctance is believed to be influenced by both heredity and early learning experiences.

Outlook:

Desurgent call reluctance, given sufficient time, accurate diagnosis, and proper training procedures is both preventable and correctable.

CareerStyle:
- May seem cold, distant and emotionally unresponsive to superficial observers
- Tend to over-analyze and under-act
- Reserved and emotionally self-restrained
- Preoccupied with being absolutely prepared for each sales call
- Sales presentations tend to stress information while neglecting emotion
- Place high value upon realism and objectivity
- Very difficult to impress (like protensives, but for different reasons)
- Tend to excel in one-on-one sales situations
- Consider motivational/inspirational management techniques unprofessional, superficial and demotivating
- Tend to have encyclopedic product knowledge
- Reflective and contemplative
- Consider themselves to be very private people
- Refuse to self-disclose, then feel like nobody really knows or understands them
- Slow to take action
- Do not like to be physically touched in public
- Tend to be comfortable with computers, systems and procedures
- Incorrectly considered to be unmotivated
- Smother their sales calls with too much sales support material
- Cynical about the value of interpersonal or rapport-building sales training procedures
- Will not visibly show excitement about a new product or program

- Suspect the motives of people who "smile too much"
- Threatened by sales training that involves role-playing
- Demotivated by inspirational pep-talks
- Exaggerate the role of organization and planning to such a point that it becomes limiting

Self-Assessment:

- Do you tend to censor yourself from expressing what you really feel about others and how much you feel it? (Desurgents are aware of frequently censoring their feelings.)

- Do you think that public displays of emotion are signs of character weakness, lack of self-control or insincerity? (Desurgents act like they are.)

- Do you have a ready, exuberant sense of humor? (Desurgents tend to have a less accessible, drier sense of humor.)

- When would it be appropriate to express emotions like joy or sorrow in a business situation? (Desurgents come up with a *long* list of conditions.)

- Do you tend to touch people you are talking to? (Desurgents consider it forward, insincere, superficial and socially improper.)

- Do you ever discuss sex, religion or politics with people *shortly* after meeting them? (Desurgents consider these subjects too personal. They wait five years.)

- Do you tend to daydream about being in highly emotional situations where you are swept away by the intensity of the moment without regard for what is proper or expected? (Desurgents compensate for their rigid, emotional self-control by frequently allowing their feelings to express themselves without constraint in their *imaginations*.)

Objective Assessments:

Call Reluctance Scale
A high prospecting Brake Score plus a high DSY score indicates that desurgent call reluctance is probably limiting prospecting performance now.

A low prospecting Brake Score plus a high DSY score indicates a predisposition to desurgent call reluctance although it is probably *not* limiting prospecting performance at the present time.

Selling Style Profile Analysis

Desurgent salespeople tend to be product-oriented in their sales presentation style.

Sales Profile Analysis

Sales forecasting tests, like the Sales Profile Analysis, project desurgent salespeople to produce at better-than-average levels, but to take longer than average to get there due to the emotional ceiling on their prospecting activity.

Frequency of Occurrence:

Desurgent call reluctance is the most frequent form of call reluctance found in technical salespeople. It is the second most frequently observed type overall.

Most Effective Treatments:

Thought Realignment
Thought Zapping
Fear Inversion

Protension

Abbreviation: L

Capsule Summary:

Protensive call reluctance occurs in salespeople who try to compensate for suspicions they hold about their own personal value by overinvesting in the *appearances and mannerisms* of worth, accomplishment and ability. To distract themselves from the real issue, their personal worth, they become preoccupied with ostentatious displays of the *symbols* of success. But projecting a successful image is just the first step. The image must then be vigilantly *defended and protected at all cost*. To do this, they must assume a constant emotional readiness to snuff out any real or imagined affront or threat to their self-merchandised dignity and respect. Prospecting, in the ordinary sense of the word, is emotionally out of the question. To them, it is just *hustling* which they see as demeaning, undignified and beneath them. So they refuse to do it. Instead, they concentrate exclusively on one or two large, low-probability cases and unproven prospecting methods which they insist are more compatible with their temperament and professional image. The result is a shallow or nonexistent client base.

Probable Origins:

Protension is a technical term taken from an internationally used personality test called the Sixteen Personality Factors Questionnaire (16PF). In 16PF studies, it is abbreviated with the letter "L" to reflect the order in which the factor was originally discovered. The word "protension" is formed by compacting two other words, "projection" (a psychological defense mechanism) and "inner-tension" (or emotional agitation). Thus, the word technically means the projection of *inner*-tension onto the *outside* world. Protensive call reluctance was discovered by observing and refining the measurement of prospecting avoidance behavior found in salespeople and sales managers with high protension scores on the 16PF. It is considered one of the "big three" forms that call reluctance can take due to the difficulty that protensive salespeople have *admitting they have a performance-limiting problem*. To them, it's always somebody else's problem. The protensive *personality*, as measured by the 16PF, probably has a modest hereditary connection. Protensive *call reluctance*, however, seems to be precipitated by active and passive learning.

Protension is Not Dominance

Managers and consultants typically mistake protension for dominance. They look the same on many grid-like rating scales. Protension easily outwits the efforts of many celebrated pop-psych tests to detect it. The two behavioral dimensions—dominance and protension—share some characteristics which make accurate assessment difficult. But there are several very important differences for every benign similarity.

Dominance, when properly measured, is personality-based forcefulness. Protension is recoil. If you are a dominant salesperson, you struggle up the side of a mountain whistling, "Mama don't let your babies grow up to be cowboys," because you are exhilarated by the sensation of challenge. If you're protensive, however, the climb is tougher. You try to *look* cool while you *scheme* your way to the top whistling Mozart, looking back over your shoulder to check where the competition is, making excuses every time you stumble, and threatening everything that gets in your way.

Dominant salespeople want to do the best they can because they enjoy accomplishment and overpowering obstacles. Win or lose, they enjoy the struggle. Protensive salespeople are involved in another enterprise altogether. They believe that they have to be the very best or they are nothing at all. One derives satisfaction from the effort itself, the other copes with self-imposed pressure and dreads the humiliation of failure. To the unskilled observer, both just appear to be climbing the mountainside.

Outlook:

The outlook for protensive call reluctance depends entirely upon *self-responsibility*. If you are able to *admit* to yourself that you may have protensive call reluctance, then the outlook for you is bright indeed. The outlook is not so optimistic if you are unable to admit the presence of performance-limiting problems, such as protensive call reluctance. Nevertheless, two procedures in this book, Thought Realignment and Fear Inversion, could be just what your career needs. Keep reading. Give them a try.

CareerStyle:

- Consider themselves to be multi-faceted conversationalists
- Tend to be obsessed with making strong, favorable first impressions
- Emotionally, they must be right all the time, even when wrong
- Do not like to have to *prove* mastery of presentation content to management or anyone else
- Cope with their own mistakes by blaming and denial
- Dislike making sales calls with management
- Women wear designer clothes and pretentious jewelry
- Men tend to have neatly trimmed beards, wear a Rolex, and, if they smoke, smoke imported cigars or affected pipes
- Compelled to critique the quality of movies, cars, clothes, cameras, computers, cuisine and wines
- Defensive and tend to snarl when they are offended or disagree with something
- Pretentious and display affected mannerisms
- May seem easy-going, caring and accessible on the surface, but are tight and angry just beneath
- Some may have a problem controlling smoking or drinking
- May speak with soft, over-stated gentleness to conceal their impatient and demanding natures

- Become over-extended in professional or industry organizations
- Hold grudges and are motivated by anger and vengeance
- Mortified by the fear of being exposed or humiliated
- May use intimidation to manipulate and control others
- Refuse to be considered average on anything
- Need to be considered the smartest and most perceptive
- Threatened by sophisticated, objective personality tests; get critical and defensive when asked to complete them
- Love to manipulate sophisticated interviewers
- Criticize more than they compliment
- Very difficult to impress (like desurgent, but for different reasons)
- Have mastered the art of faking through most tests and all interviews
- Have trouble honestly self-disclosing (fear loss of approval if people really know them)
- Big case-itis (only work on big dollar, low probability prospective sales)
- Obsessed with credibility
- Pretentiously decorate their offices with plaques, certificates, awards and other status-declarative references to achievement and character
- Quick to blame management, training, the company and its products, advertising and sales supports for their personal lack of verifiable sales performance (which is really due to their refusal to initiate contact with prospective buyers in sufficient numbers)
- Compulsive name-droppers
- Secretly jealous and envious of the success earned by co-workers
- Like to gossip
- Office snipers
- Not emotionally able to allow anyone to train, teach, advise or counsel them
- May drive an expensive automobile to make an impression, not for enjoyment
- Order special license tags which read "No. One" or "Stud"

- Do not find lasting satisfaction in people or things
- Make exceptionally strong and favorable first impression
- Tend to have large vocabularies

Self-Assessment:

- Are you always on the lookout for alternative and more professional ways to prospect in lieu of proven prospecting methods? (If you have protensive call reluctance, you spend your time searching for other ways to prospect instead of actually prospecting.)
- Do you always tend to have to add something, subtract something, amend or modify what someone says when they are trying to teach you?
- Do you tend to react emotionally (especially defensively) whenever someone doubts your competency or your integrity?
- Do you tend to buy expensive things which don't satisfy you for very long?
- When you are asked to complete an objective personality test, do you discredit the nature of the test, scribble unsolicited commentary (usually negative) on the test booklet or answer sheet, ignore questions you don't agree with (despite instructions to answer every question), or just refuse to complete the test? (Salespeople with protensive call reluctance seem to be unable to control the impulse to criticize and critique. This becomes particularly noticeable in their test-taking behavior. They inject self-protecting unsolicited critical comments about the test or certain test questions, or in some rare cases they refuse to complete the test altogether. Despite how they answer the actual test questions, their test-taking *behavior* reveals their protensive call reluctance.)
- How important is a salesperson's appearance to his or her success? (Salespeople with protensive call reluctance believe it is a determining factor. Non-protensives believe that having it is important if and only if other things like prospecting are done.)
- Do you tend to have a cynical, sarcastic or cutting sense of humor? (Salespeople with protensive call reluctance do.)

Objective Assessments:

Call Reluctance Scale

A high prospecting Brake Score plus a high L score indicates that protensive call reluctance is probably limiting prospecting activity now.

A low prospecting Brake Score plus a high L score indicates a predisposition to protensive call reluctance although it is probably not limiting prospecting performance at the present time.

Selling Styles Profile Analysis
Salespeople with protensive call reluctance tend to be image-oriented in their sales presentation style.

Sales Profile Analysis
Sales forecasting tests, like the Sales Profile Analysis, project salespeople with protensive call reluctance to produce at marginal levels of performance while taking shorter-than-average times to reach this level and requiring higher-than-average investments of management time, money and effort. When protensive call reluctance is corrected, however, these salespeople are often counted among the most talented and productive members of the sales force.

Frequency of Occurrence:

Protensive call reluctance is the fifth most frequently occurring type of call reluctance in salespeople.

Most Effective Treatments:

Thought Realignment
Thought Zapping
Fear Inversion

Groups

Abbreviation: GPS

Capsule Summary:

Fear of speaking before a group is a facet of call reluctance which occurs in salespeople who are overanxious about appearance, approval and acceptance. They may be comfortable self-promoting in one-on-one situations but become distressed in front of groups. Some are able to handle small groups but not large ones. Some are emotionally uncomfortable in front of large and small groups. This form of call reluctance has no noticeable impact in industries where prospecting is traditionally done through non-group channels. In other industries, where "seminar" and "party" selling is emphasized, group call reluctance can be catastrophic.

Probable Origin:

Group call reluctance appears to be entirely learned. It may come from inexperience as a group speaker or from an early traumatic experience giving a group presentation. There is sketchy evidence that the "fight or flight" response experienced by salespeople with group call reluctance may be due to body chemistry. Some very recent research for example indicates that the prescription drug propanolol may be able to block these distressful feelings at their chemical source. The drug, however, has several noteworthy side effects, including possible death.

Outlook:

Group call reluctance is among the easiest to correct when it is properly assessed and the proper training supports are used.

CareerStyle:

- Even an *imagined* presentation in front of a group is accompanied by signs of distress
- Preparation and worrying begin weeks before group presentations are to be given
- Opportunities for group presentations are avoided
- Read only those books related to the problem which do not require actual presentations to be given
- Drop out early from remedial activities to avoid having to speak before groups
- Over-prepare notes, even for short informal situations like introductions or *spontaneous* remarks in a group setting
- Dread "ice-breaking" activities like standing up and giving their names
- Allow markets that are most reachable through seminar selling to wither away or pass to a competitor
- Read notes verbatim when forced to speak before a group

- Secretly dread role-playing in training situations
- May cope by being either too cautious or too cavalier when in front of a group

Self-Assessment:

- Do you actively seek out opportunities to go before groups of various sizes to promote yourself? (Salespeople with group call reluctance never do.)

- Do you tend to be self-critical when you hear yourself on tape or see yourself on video? (Salespeople with group call reluctance really get down on themselves.)

- Do you secretly rehearse "spontaneous" words and actions in your mind prior to speaking before a group? (Salespeople with group call reluctance do.)

- Do you tend to think that every speaker you hear is much better than you could ever be no matter how hard you worked at it? (Salespeople with group call reluctance are convinced that they could never be comfortable or effective in front of others.)

- Do you tend to daydream about giving powerful religious or political orations, or acting in films or on the stage?

Objective Assessments:

Call Reluctance Scale
A high prospecting Brake Score plus a high GPS score indicates that group call reluctance could be limiting prospecting performance at the present time if prospecting channels include seminar or group presentations.

A low prospecting Brake Score plus a high GPS score indicates a predisposition to group call reluctance although it is probably not limiting prospecting performance at the present time.

Selling Styles Profile Analysis
Salespeople with group call reluctance have a slight tendency to be service-oriented in their sales presentation style.

Sales Profile Analysis
Sales forecasting tests, like the Sales Profile Analysis, project low-to-average performance for salespeople with group call reluctance *if they are in a sales setting where they have to speak before groups.*

Frequency of Occurrence:

Group call reluctance is the sixth most frequently observed type found in salespeople. It's incidence is estimated to be much greater among non-salespeople.

Most Effective Treatments:

Thought Realignment
Threat Desensitization

Friends

Abbreviation: FRN

Capsule Summary:

Friends call reluctance occurs when salespeople become too protective about how their friends might react if they were to make a sales call on them, or ask them for referrals. Friends call reluctance is a natural emotional reaction to doubts that these salespeople have about the depth and quality of their friendships. They believe that their friends would be offended and feel exploited if they made a sales presentation to them. So to avoid the loss of approval and to protect their friendships, making sales calls on their friends is ruled emotionally out of bounds. Regrettably, the competition does not recognize these emotional boundaries.

Probable Origin:

Friends call reluctance is learned. It may be acquired through exposure to passive stereotypes about selling, friendships, or both. In either case, it is easily corrected once it is properly detected and the right procedures are used.

Friends call reluctance has only a modest relationship to family call reluctance (a structurally similar form which places the family emotionally off limits). The correlation between the two is not high. They are psychologically separate and distinct entities. A salesperson having friends call reluctance is no more likely to have family call reluctance than any other type. Friends call reluctance is much more likely to be related to *Role Acceptance*, another form of call reluctance which consists of unexpressed guilt and shame associated with being in sales. With friends call reluctance, the salesperson reacts to his friends as if they hold his sales career in the same low esteem that he does.

Outlook:

Friends call reluctance is easy to correct if it is properly detected and the appropriate training procedures are used.

CareerStyle:
- Never refer to business when around friends
- Try to conceal emotional discomfort by convincing other salespeople that calling on friends is unethical and unprofessional
- Take longer to develop a prospect base because of inability to use one of the most potent sources of referrals available, friends
- May not have a problem calling on family members
- Consider salespeople who do call on their friends to be unprofessional
- May become belligerent when asked by management to justify their position
- Never mix business and friendships
- Hesitant to give friends' names as referrals to other salespeople

Self-Assessment:
- Do you ever feel that you have to protect your friends from your managers or other salespeople in your organization? (Without realizing it, salespeople with friends call reluctance often believe they have to protect their friends from their colleagues in sales and their sales managers.)
- Do your friends know you have been protecting them from you, if in fact you have been? (Salespeople with friends call reluctance often make decisions to protect their friends from a sales presentation without first asking their friends if they want or need protection. Some of your friends might *want* to hear your sales presentation.)
- Do you try to keep your friendships and business interests absolutely separate? (Salespeople with friends call reluctance do.)
- When you talk about your work with your friends, do you purposefully deemphasize prospecting? (Salespeople with friends call reluctance don't discuss their prospecting activity with their friends.)

- Have your friends ever tried to sell you anything? Did you feel exploited by them? Did you immediately discontinue the friendship? (Most salespeople with friends call reluctance live a double standard. They allow their friends to try to sell them things like investments, insurance or real estate, but they won't allow themselves the emotional freedom to reciprocate.)

Objective Assessments:

Call Reluctance Scale

A high prospecting Brake Score plus a high FRN score indicates that friends call reluctance is probably limiting prospecting performance at the present time.

A low prospecting Brake Score plus a high FRN score indicates a predisposition to friends call reluctance although it is probably not limiting prospecting performance at the present time.

Selling Styles Profile Analysis

Salespeople with friends call reluctance do not have a dominant characteristic selling style.

Sales Profile Analysis

Sales forecasting tests, like the Sales Profile Analysis, project salespeople with friends call reluctance to take longer-than-average to reach production potential due to the emotional difficulty they have utilizing a primary source of sales and referrals.

Frequency of Occurrence:

Friends call reluctance is the fourth most frequently observed type in salespeople.

Most Effective Treatments:

Thought Realignment
Thought Zapping
Logical Persuasion (a general support procedure which is not included in this book but which is readily available elsewhere)

Role Acceptance

Abbreviation: ROL

Capsule Summary:

Role acceptance call reluctance occurs when salespeople believe they ought to be in a career other than sales. Often they believe they are a disappointment to some significant person in their lives such as their mother or father. This results in an unexpressed residue of guilt and shame which makes it impossible for them to derive satisfaction from their careers or to feel good about seizing opportunities to prospect with *genuine* energy and zeal.

Probable Origin:

Role Acceptance is learned. The seeds for it are sown by early learning experiences long before entering sales. It's a part of the emotional baggage salespeople bring with them to the sales career. After entering a sales career, it is precipitated by production quotas, sales training experiences and other performance pressures.

We conducted a study several years ago using the Motivation Analysis Test and other measurements to assess the kinds and degrees of motivation found in terminating male life insurance agents (back then the overwhelming majority of life insurance agents were male). Each terminating agent had failed to complete his first year of tenure under contract. An astonishing number, however, terminated while performing at successful levels. They were not production failures. The loss of these salesmen was perplexing. The Motivation Analysis Test provided the key. Test results revealed that a significant number of the terminating agents had a considerable amount of conflict and emotional "unfinished business" with their parents. Informal exit interviewing corroborated this finding and added a remarkable insight. Many of them terminated because they felt pressured to do something more prestigious, to "make something of themselves." This could not include selling regardless of how much they liked it or how well they did it. When asked, many attributed the source of their pressure to parental expectations. In some of those cases, their parents had been dead for over a decade.

Outlook:

Role Acceptance is easy to correct once it is properly assessed and appropriate training procedures are used.

CareerStyle:

- Cope by being either too cautious or too cavalier
- May have episodes of depression associated with the career
- May try to conceal their feelings by pretending to be very positive
- Unable to emotionally take ownership of the career
- Never get fully into the sales career though they pretend to be involved
- Won't allow themselves to make an autonomous career choice
- Fear loss of approval from significant others
- Rarely feel genuine pride in sales accomplishments
- Fail to clearly disclose that they are in sales during opportune occasions such as civic, social, religious and fraternal gatherings where such information could help prospecting efforts
- Strongest advocates of positive attitudes
- Fragile positivism; can't stand to have negative people around them
- Unable to emotionally believe that a sales career is valid or worthwhile
- Have emotionally bought into damaging stereotypes about selling without realizing it
- Believe that society holds salespeople in justified low esteem or even contempt
- Pretending to be positive extracts energy and produces burnout
- Some compensate for negative feelings by writing books and giving speeches *about positive attitudes and uncritically advocating the validity of the sales career*

Self-Assessment:

- Do you tend to be self-deprecating when you talk to other people about your sales career? (Salespeople with role acceptance problems act like their careers are inferior to other people's.)
- Do you tend to be rigidly positive when you are around your sales colleagues? (Salespeople with role acceptance problems tend to act just the opposite when around other salespeople. They appear to be the most positive, zealous and committed salespeople in the business.)

Consultants with Role Acceptance Call Reluctance

Watch who you let near your mind. Role acceptance call reluctance is highly contagious. Be wary of consultants who are selling sales training programs, but who themselves are unable to accept the fact that *they are also salespeople.* Here's a quick check. Ask your prospective consultant if he or she considers him/herself to be a *good* salesperson. Don't get sidetracked by the subjective definition of "good." That's a tactical evasion. If they say *anything* that indicates an emotional denial of their sales role like, "Oh no, *I'm* not really a salesperson," open the door and close your mind, fast.

- Are your positive attitudes contrived? (Salespeople with role acceptance call reluctance must force themselves to act as if they are positive.)

- Does your mood about your sales career tend to vacillate from very high to very low? (Salespeople with role acceptance call reluctance tend to be very high on their career one moment and very low the next.)

- Do you try to find verbal replacements for the term "salesperson" when describing what you do? (Salespeople with role acceptance call reluctance presume that the term "salesperson" is *unacceptable* and try to replace it with terms which distract from the sales function, such as "financial planner," "account representative," or "territorial representative." Note: *Insistence* upon terms like these is one way that corporations *institutionalize* role acceptance problems and pass them on to their sales force.)

- Do you have to call prospecting something else before it is acceptable to you? (Salespeople with role acceptance problems tend to rely upon alternative names for prospecting such as "clientele building.")

- Have you changed sales organizations several times for reasons other than production? (Salespeople with role acceptance problems are searching for the *emotional* right to feel good about their sales career. That may take them through several organizations before they realize that what they are searching for is self-generated.)

- Do you tend to daydream about being in an important position where everyone likes you and you feel good about yourself? (Salespeople with role acceptance call reluctance enjoy taking imaginary trips to careers where the grass is always greener.)

- Have you ever moved to another city on impulse? (Some salespeople with role acceptance call reluctance are inclined to require a frequent change of locale.)

- Do you believe that if you were to upgrade your career that everyone would approve of you and you would feel better about yourself? (Salespeople with role acceptance call reluctance labor under this misconception.)

- Do you tend to latch on to one self-help philosophy after another? (Many salespeople with role acceptance call reluctance shop for intellectual solutions for their *emotional* needs.)

Objective Assessments:

Call Reluctance Scale
A high prospecting Brake Score plus a high ROL score indicates that role acceptance call reluctance is probably limiting prospecting performance at the present time.

A low prospecting Brake Score plus a high ROL score indicates a predisposition to role acceptance call reluctance although it is probably not limiting prospecting performance at the present time.

Selling Styles Profile Analysis
No significant relationships exist between this type of call reluctance and selling styles.

Sales Profile Analysis
Sales forecasting tests, like the Sales Profile Analysis, project longer-than-average time will be required to reach performance potential due to the emotional limit placed on prospecting.

Frequency of Occurrence:

Role acceptance call reluctance is the sixth most frequently observed type found in salespeople. Some industries, however, tend to have higher observed frequencies.

Most Effective Treatments:
Thought Realignment
Thought Zapping

Disruption Sensitivity

Abbreviation: DS

Capsule Summary:

Disruption sensitivity call reluctance occurs in salespeople who have difficulty asserting themselves, particularly when it comes to prospecting. Unwilling to risk being considered pushy, forward or intrusive, they continuously yield to the needs and interests of other people. In so doing, they put themselves on perpetual hold. Because prospecting is essentially an act of initiating contacts, these salespeople have trouble doing it. They are afraid that their prospective contacts might be busy or otherwise engaged. So they sacrifice their careers by waiting for the "right" time, the "right" circumstances, and for a guarantee that they will not be intruding. These conditions are never met.

Probable Origin:

Disruption sensitivity call reluctance appears to be the combined result of hereditary influences and past experiences. It surfaces when low dominance (a general personality predisposition) obstructs prospecting performance. Disruption Sensitivity is not the opposite of over-aggressiveness which is often just ineffective behavior displayed by low dominant people trying to cope.

Outlook:

Since disruption sensitivity call reluctance contains an hereditary influence, it is not easily eliminated. But if properly assessed and if the proper training procedures are used, it can be arrested and prospecting performance can be significantly improved. This outlook is further supported by the fact that most salespeople with disruption sensitivity call reluctance follow instructions and are easy to work with.

CareerStyle:

- Hesitant to express their own interests and needs
- Tend to be angry at themselves for allowing others to "walk all over them"
- Easy to persuade, sometimes gullible; accept clients' objections too quickly
- Vulnerable to close reluctance

- Over-emphasize the rapport-building, relationship-oriented elements of the sales process at the expense of assertive prospecting and closing
- Refuse to be more aggressive; become indignant at the suggestion
- Consider aggressive salespeople and managers to be unprofessional
- Have difficulty expressing anger, so it builds up inside
- Defer to the needs of others, bankrupts own interests
- Tend to be very warm and sociable
- Manipulate others through non-confrontational means, such as gossiping and strategic complaining
- Mentally resolved to be more assertive but unable to carry it out behaviorally

Self-Assessment:

- Do you often feel like people take advantage of you? (Disruption sensitive salespeople often feel that way.)
- When you recognize that people are taking advantage of you, do you still find it difficult to do anything about it? (Salespeople with disruption sensitivity call reluctance find it difficult.)
- Is it hard for you to talk when you get angry? (Disruption sensitive salespeople are so concerned about managing their anger and keeping it all locked away inside that they can hardly talk to the people who upset them.)
- Were you taught as a child never to be too forward, and that being forward was the same as being selfish? (Salespeople with disruption sensitivity call reluctance confuse asserting their own interests with being forward, and being forward with being bad.)
- Do you consider yourself a gentle person? (Disruption sensitive salespeople tend to be gentle people.)
- How difficult would it be for you to handle a prospective client who called you pushy and rude? (It would require two weeks of hospitalization for salespeople with Disruption Sensitivity.)
- Is using the telephone to prospect more difficult than face-to-face prospecting? (It is for salespeople with disruption sensitivity call reluctance.)
- Have you ever called yourself a "wimp?" (Salespeople with Disruption Sensitivity tend to call themselves worse names than that.)

- Do you have "command and control" daydreams where you are in a position to issue orders and take decisive actions which assert a dramatic impact on the people and situations around you? (Disruption sensitive salespeople tend to enjoy this kind of daydreaming.)

- When you talk to people who you are comfortable with, do you tend to exaggerate how you handled a conflict, stood up to someone, or issued an ultimatum that your position be adhered to? (Disruption sensitive salespeople often tell tall tales of assertive victories which never really occurred.)

Objective Assessments:

Call Reluctance Scale
A high prospecting Brake Score plus high DS score indicates that disruption sensitivity call reluctance could be limiting prospecting performance at the present time.

A low prospecting Brake Score plus a high DS score indicates a predisposition to disruption sensitivity call reluctance although it is probably not limiting prospecting performance at the present time.

Selling Styles Profile Analysis
Salespeople with disruption sensitivity call reluctance have a strong tendency to be rapport-oriented. They stress the interpersonal elements of the sales process.

Sales Profile Analysis
Sales forecasting tests, like the Sales Profile Analysis, project disruption sensitive salespeople to produce at average levels and to take longer-than-average to reach that level due to the emotional constraints they place on prospecting.

Frequency of Occurrence:

Disruption Sensitivity is the most frequently observed type of call reluctance found in salespeople regardless of industry or sales setting.

Most Effective Treatments:

Thought Realignment
Assertion Training (general procedure not contained in this book but readily available elsewhere)

Social Differential

Abbreviation: SD

Capsule Summary:

Social Differential is a highly targeted form of call reluctance. Salespeople who have it can usually initiate contact with anyone *unless* they are a member of a group they have selected to avoid for emotional reasons. It occurs in salespeople who are too socially self-conscious. They labor under a rigid, self-imposed psychological caste system which elevates people who have education, position or wealth to levels of superiority the salesperson *emotionally* considers out of his or her reach. When in the presence of such people, salespeople with social differential call reluctance allow themselves to be easily intimidated. They cope by simply avoiding contact.

Probable Origin:

Social differential call reluctance is acquired through passive learning. It is highly contagious. Typically, it is spread by sales managers, trainers, consultants or implicit messages embedded within the sales training process itself. Often it is confused with low self-esteem and low assertiveness which are more related to other forms of call reluctance.

Outlook:

Social Differential is one of the most limiting forms that call reluctance can take. When a company shifts its marketing emphasis to up-market clientele, or when purchasing decisions for a product or service are made at high organizational levels, or when educated professional people constitute the prime market for a product or service, social differential call reluctance can be lethal. However, if it is detected early and the proper training is provided, it is among the easiest and fastest forms of call reluctance to correct.

CareerStyle:

- Most common form of call reluctance found in veteran salespeople
- Limits experienced salespeople to certain production plateaus for extended periods of time
- Limits prospecting activity to salesperson's own, or lower, socio-economic groups

- Change sales organizations frequently to avoid up-market sales and marketing campaigns

- Able to prospect without difficulty in every area except up-market and professional sectors

- When asked to justify position they simply say, "I don't call on *them*", and give no reason why

- Shoot at wrong targets, typically giving their presentations to non-decision makers in corporate sales situations

- Assume submissive, childlike behaviors when in the presence of people they perceive to be powerful, authoritative or parental

- Looks like low motivation or poor goal direction to the uninitiated

- Addicted to esteem-building self-help material

- May have come from blue collar backgrounds

- Some tend to be abusive, impatient, tyrannical and intimidating to other people who they perceive to be lower on the caste system than themselves, such as secretaries and maintenance personnel

- Embellish and exaggerate the power, fame and money of the people who intimidate them when discussing them with friends and co-workers

- Plan to make more up-market contacts during goal-setting sessions but are never able to translate plans into consistent prospecting practices

Self-Assessment:

- Do you tend to be more childlike when in the presence of certain people, such as physicians, clergymen and senior corporate officials? (Salespeople with social differential call reluctance tend to be in-gratiating when in the presence of such people.)

- Are you ever rude or pretend to be too busy when you interact with vendors at conventions, or when other salespeople call on you? (Salespeople with social differential call reluctance tend to in-timidate other salespeople when they are in position to do so; and do so in *exactly the same way they feel that people in power and control intimidate them.*)

- Is it critical that other people think you are important? (It is to salespeople who have social differential call reluctance.)

- Do you know a lot of up-market professional people that you could contact but haven't? (If you have social differential call reluctance, you probably know several.)

- Do you get secretly angry with yourself for being so easy to intimidate? (Salespeople with social differential call reluctance do.)

- Do you daydream about being a member of a prestigious profession or the head of a large corporation where you have uncontested power? (Salespeople with social differential call reluctance dream of worlds where they are in a position of wealth, prestige and power.)

Objective Assessments:

Call Reluctance Scale
A high prospecting Brake Score plus a high SD score indicates that social differential call reluctance is probably limiting prospecting performance at the present time.

A low prospecting Brake Score plus a high SD score indicates a predisposition to social differential call reluctance although it is probably not limiting prospecting performance at the present time.

Selling Styles Profile Analysis
Salespeople with social differential call reluctance tend to be either close-oriented or service-oriented.

Sales Profile Analysis
Depending upon market setting, sales forecasting tests like the Sales Profile Analysis, project salespeople with social differential call reluctance to reach average levels of production early and remain there until their emotional resistance to up-market prospecting is removed.

Frequency of Occurrence:

Social Differential is the seventh most frequently observed type of call reluctance found in salespeople. However, it is only performance-limiting in industries where calling on up-market clientele is required.

Most Effective Treatments:

Thought Realignment
Thought Zapping
Negative Image Projection

Logical Problem Solving (a general procedure not provided in this book because it is readily available elsewhere)

Family/Relatives

Abbreviation: FAM

Capsule Summary:

Family/relative call reluctance occurs in salespeople who are not emotionally emancipated from their parents. Adult-like in other respects, they tend to regress to perceptions, emotions and behaviors they knew as children when they are around their parents and relatives. There, they are still children. They believe that trying to prospect among the members of their own family would never work. It would involve risking parental rejection and disapproval. Their kin would be justifiably offended and feel exploited. Worst of all, they wouldn't take a sales presentation seriously if it was given by a salesperson they knew as a naughty child and a fumbling adolescent.

Probable Origin:

Family/relative call reluctance is acquired through active and passive learning. Predisposition to it usually originates long before entry into the sales career. Often, this includes frequent exposure to negative stereotypes held by family members about selling and salespeople. Once in sales, it is unintentionally worsened by sales management or the sales training process.

Family/relative call reluctance has only a modest relationship to friends call reluctance (a structurally similar form which places personal friends emotionally off limits). The correlation between the two is not high. They are psychologically separate and distinct entities. A salesperson having family/relative call reluctance is no more likely to have friends call reluctance than any other type.

Outlook:

Family/relative call reluctance is easy to correct once it has been properly detected and exposed to appropriate training procedures.

CareerStyle:

- Consider family members emotionally off limits

- Hesitate to even ask relatives for referrals
- To save face, argue that calling on family members is always un-professional and unethical
- May have no difficulty calling on personal friends
- May take longer to develop a client base due to their refusal to use one of the most potent and accessible referral sources, the family
- May regress into emotionalism (such as anger or belligerence) when asked to justify their position
- Consider salespeople who do prospect among their own family members to be exploitative and unprofessional
- Believe in never mixing business and family
- Refuse to give names of family members to other salespeople for use as referrals
- More emotionally volatile when around family members
- Feel the need to insulate family members from their career

Self-Assessment:

- Do you ever feel that you have to protect the members of your own family from your manager and the other salespeople in your organization? (Salespeople with family call reluctance go to great lengths to keep them apart.)
- Do the members of your family know that you have been insulating them from you, if in fact you have been? (Salespeople with family call reluctance rarely discuss any significant aspect of their careers with family members.)
- Did a member of your family ever try to sell you anything? If so, how did you feel about it? (Salespeople with family call reluctance tend to live a double standard. They can allow members of their family to try to sell them insurance, real estate or investments, but are unable to allow themselves the freedom to do the same).
- In general, do you tend to keep a lot of secrets from the members of your family? (Salespeople with family call reluctance tend to live two lifestyles. One is the adult lifestyle lived away from their family and which is largely unknown to their family. The other is the childlike lifestyle which is familiar to and expected by family members.)

- Would you hesitate to give a sales presentation to members of your own family even if they requested it? (Some salespeople with family call reluctance would even hesitate to do that.)

- Do you daydream about doing things which would never be accepted or understood by the members of your family? (Salespeople with family call reluctance assert their autonomy as an adult in their daydreams and fantasies.)

Objective Assessments:

Call Reluctance Scale
A high prospecting Brake Score plus a high FAM score indicates that family/relative call reluctance could be limiting prospecting performance at the present time.

A low prospecting Brake Score plus a high FAM score indicates a predisposition to family/relative call reluctance although it is probably not limiting prospecting performance at the present time.

Selling Styles Profile Analysis
Salespeople with family/relative call reluctance do not have a single characteristic selling style.

Sales Profile Analysis
Sales forecasting tests, like the Sales Profile Analysis, project salespeople with family call reluctance to take longer-than-average to reach their production potential due to the emotional difficulty in utilizing a primary source for initial sales and referrals. Note: this conclusion does not apply to telemarketers or salespeople who do not have access to the members of their families.

Frequency of Occurrence:

Family/relative call reluctance is the third most frequently observed type among all salespeople.

Most Effective Treatments:

Thought Realignment
Thought Zapping
Logical Persuasion (a general procedure not provided in this book but readily available elsewhere)

Why "Type" is Important to You

Determining the type of call reluctance you may have, or be predisposed to, is extremely important. The corrective procedures which follow are assigned by type. Applying the wrong procedure to the wrong type of call reluctance could easily make the problem worse. Let's return again to our opening case examples. We now know that Nancy had threat sensitivity call reluctance. Two procedures, Thought Realignment and Threat Desensitization, are specifically prescribed for that type. Other procedures, even those in this book, could make her problem worse, not better. Bob has both family and friends call reluctance. Both of these are easy to correct if Bob uses two special procedures, Thought Realignment and Thought Zapping. A third general procedure, Logical Persuasion, could also be used by Bob's manager as a supplement, but not as a replacement. Larry, the computer salesman, has social differential call reluctance, a condition which responds quickly to Thought Realignment, Thought Zapping and Negative Image Projection. Logical Persuasion can also be used by Larry's managers as a fourth, supplemental procedure after the primary procedures have had a chance to work.

The next section of this book consists of step-by-step procedures for correcting call reluctance. You can apply them yourself, although you would derive extra strength from a manager or colleague who agreed to serve as a source of support.

To use the *Prescriptions* section effectively, you have to do certain things in their proper order. First, you should evaluate your prospecting *activity*. Is it consistent with your desire to succeed, your talent, and the potential of your market? If it is, you may have a problem but it's not prospecting. If it's not, you may have a prospecting problem, but it's not *necessarily* call reluctance. So review the impostors. Do you have the motivation and goals necessary to have authentic call reluctance? If not, you're an impostor. Consider using some of the resources outlined at the end of Chapter Two. If your answer was "yes," then you probably have authentic call reluctance. But what *type* do you have? Review the nine types and determine which type(s) seems to fit your experience best. (Rarely does a salesperson have more than two or three types at one time.) If you have more than one type, choose the most bothersome to begin with. Then turn to the *Most Effective Treatments* provided at the end of the description for each type. If there is more than one procedure listed, go through them in *the order they are listed*. The rest is easy. Just read through the procedures and *follow the instructions*.

2

THE
PRESCRIPTIONS
℞

What you say to yourself about prospecting has a powerful impact upon what you feel when prospecting. What you feel when prospecting has a powerful impact on what you do about prospecting.

R̽ ONE

THOUGHT REALIGNMENT

PRIMARILY AFFECTS:	PRESCRIBED FOR:
X Thoughts	X Threat Sensitivity
	X Desurgency
Feelings	X Protension
	X Groups
Actions	X Personal Friends
	X Disruption Sensitivity
	X Social Differential
	X Role Acceptance
	X Family/Relatives

A BRIEF OVERVIEW

Thought Realignment is an easy-to-learn, three-step procedure. You will first learn to identify counter-productive messages hidden in the way you describe prospecting to yourself. You will then learn to control feelings which interfere with prospecting by changing your description of prospecting. And finally, you will apply what you have learned by intentionally putting yourself into emotionally difficult prospecting situations *while you practice emotional self-management skills which support your career goals.*

Guiding Principles
Behind Thought Realignment

1. *You are motivated* to improve.

2. *Your motivation is directed* specifically towards reducing unwanted distressful feelings associated with self-promotion in order to improve your prospecting activity.

3. Your feelings can either *enhance* or *impede* the flow of motivation into goal-directed behavior.

4. What you *think* about something influences how you *feel* about it.

5. Counterproductive feelings which accompany prospecting are *learned* and can be *unlearned.*

Sighting the Target

Thought Realignment is useful for both *preventing* and *correcting* all forms of the fear of self-promotion.

Estimated Completion Time

Learning to identify how thoughts and feelings can limit prospecting performance takes most salespeople only two to three hours. Developing new automatic mental management skills takes a few days of attention and practice. Detraumatizing call reluctant feelings takes about two weeks of application and practice *in actual prospecting situations* which tend to be emotionally difficult.

Some salespeople who use this procedure are able to make substantial gains in the first few hours. Others take a little longer for the information to sink in and become "real" for them.

PART ONE:
THE UNALIGNED SALESPERSON

Every car runs more smoothly when its wheel alignment is inspected periodically and adjusted when necessary. The purpose of a wheel alignment is to make sure that all the wheels point in exactly the same direction. When the steering wheel is in a position to drive straight ahead, the road wheels should be pointed in that direction. When they are not, you experience energy-robbing bumps and vibrations which feel like they are coming from the road. But they are not. They are coming from a steering wheel aimed in one direction and road wheels trying to go in another. If misalignment is not corrected, wear and tear on the car will be accelerated. Major damage eventually results when symptoms of misalignment are ignored.

Motivated, goal-directed salespeople are like cars. Sometimes their motivation tries to steer them straight ahead towards their goals, while a few renegade thoughts exert a counter force which tries to pull them off the road. When that happens, it is experienced in the form of goal-disruptive feelings, or call reluctance. Wear and tear results. If misalignment is not corrected, serious damage to the career can be expected.

Tales of Terror

Consider the following prospecting situations taken from actual Call Reluctance Center files.

Real Estate: The Hour of Doom

It's 6:55 on Wednesday evening. Each of the agents in the Jack L. Smith Real Estate Agency knows that in five minutes it will be time to start using the phone to prospect for new listings. One agent, the newest, becomes progressively more frightened as the time draws nearer. Another, a veteran agent, shows predictable signs of anger. A third begins to look deflated and depressed. A fourth projects a practiced, knowing, cynical half-smile.

Insurance: The Haunting

Times are changing. Larry G, a veteran insurance agent for a high visibility agency in the Northeast, is preparing for his first prospecting seminar. He knows the product, has years of experience under his belt, and is highly motivated to come away from the experience with several new clients. But as the hour approaches, he becomes more and more distressed. There's more. In his industry, he is well-known as one of the "most dynamic advocates" of a positive mental outlook. Recently when he spoke at an industry convention, he strongly argued that "if you can conceive it, you can have it." But now Larry's up against the wall. His hands are clammy, his pupils dilated, and his knees are shaking. It's making a mockery of everything he values and stands for. He's beginning to wonder if the whole enterprise might be a mistake.

Office Equipment: Spirits in the Boardroom

Phyllis K is a seasoned sales veteran. She has sold computer software, encyclopedias, and now copying machines. She knows her product. She knows how to sell it. She recently presented her product to a personnel manager who wants it, and to the company's purchasing manager who has tentatively approved its purchase. There is only one hurdle left. Now, because of the large dollar amount of the sale, she must give her presentation to four senior officers, *in the boardroom*. For Phyllis, the whole thing takes on a different look. As she approaches the boardroom, she senses a vague internal struggle to retain her characteristic self-confidence. But the closer she gets, the harder it is to keep it all together. Finally, when she enters the room it becomes obvious to everyone that she is *coping*, not selling. She has successfully gone through this process a hundred times with owners of small and moderate-sized businesses. The opportunity to close a really big sale approaches, but the presentation switches to a boardroom and the prospects are executive officers of a large organization. That changes the complexion for Phyllis. She knows she's trying too hard. Talking too much. She overstates. Cuts the competition. Seems boastful and over-confident. Even defensive. Ultimately, she will lose this sale. She will lose it because *she was unable to manage herself* in an up-market sales situation.

What happened? Why did these salespeople sabotage their opportunities to move closer to their production goals? Let's find out.

THE ROLE OF FEELINGS

We assign meaning to each person, place, situation or thing we perceive. Research scientists have been trying for a long time to discover exactly how we do this. To date, they have learned much. But more remains to be learned. So where do we venture from here? And how do we get there?

One way to begin piecing together an understanding of the meanings behind our feelings is to use a speculative license called a *conceptual model*. Models are helpful because they allow theoreticians and practitioners to proceed from a point of ignorance *as if they know something they really don't*. At present, there are several good models aspiring to explain where feelings come from. Each has its own strengths and weaknesses. Our version approaches the problem from the unique perspective of call reluctance.

When a Rose is Not a Rose

If you were a perfect computer, you would process information by carrying out the steps you were programmed to perform, and you would do it the same way every time. Nothing added. Nothing taken away. You would execute commands you recognized from your programmed experience. You would ignore or refuse to ponder commands you did not recognize. Simple. Elegant. But not human.

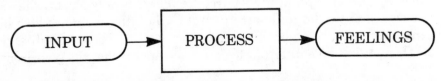

As a human being, when you get a parcel of information from inside or outside yourself, you respond similar to a computer and you rush to process it. But here you part company with computers. You do not dash straight ahead in objective, predictable order. Instead, you hang a screeching hard left at the first intersection and proceed down Subjective Avenue to the Personal Meaning Check-In Station. There, all incoming information is frisked and subjected to three *filters*. Based on the results, you begin the process of selecting 1) *how* you will feel, and 2) *how much* you will feel it.

One of the filters waiting to process incoming traffic is *past experience*. It compares incoming information with prior records. A horsewhip might cast a smile on your face if you pleasantly recall the sounds and sights of crisp autumn horse-and-buggy rides from your childhood. *But what if your parents used a horsewhip for disciplinary purposes when you were a child?*

Present needs is another filter. It tilts our perceptions towards the things we need at the moment. You might not even notice a restaurant as you drive by if you have just finished a hearty meal. *But what if it's been two days since you last ate?*

The last filter consists of your *values*. It has to do with what you consider to be right and wrong, good and bad. You might see an offer of brandy as a kindly warm-up for a cold winter's night. *But how would you respond if you strongly believed that alcohol consumption was inherently evil and spiritually corrupting?*

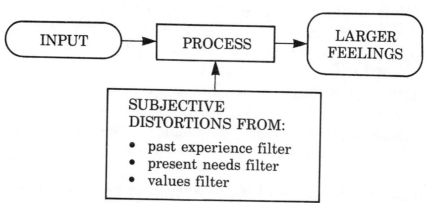

A now classic research study illustrates our model. Ten-year-olds from rich and poor backgrounds were asked to estimate the size of a coin which they held in their hands. According to the study, "When the results for rich and poor children were looked at separately, it was found that the poor children overestimated the size of the coin more than the rich children." Why? Can the "perceptual filtering" model you have just learned help explain these results?

17 Mindbenders

Here are 17 ways you can distort your perceptions and bend your frame of mind.

1. **Reading Minds**—Believing that you are particularly perceptive about other people and that you know what they are *really* up to.

2. **Blaming**—Trying to hold other people, places and situations responsible for *your* current behavior.

3. **Ruling**—Trying to impose rigid, inflexible regimentation on yourself and others.

4. **Weighing**—Believing you can impose legalistic balance and fairness on your relationships with other people.

5. **Deferring**—Deferring too many *present* enjoyments to some distant time when everything is just right.

6. **Selecting**—Seeing only *one* aspect of a person or situation and ignoring everything else.

7. **Dooming**—Seeing only terrible, worst-case outcomes and then alarming yourself.

8. **Affecting**—Relying only on what you feel at the moment to discern the truth about another person or a situation.

9. **Informing**—Insisting that you are always *right* even in the face of contradictory evidence or inconclusive information.

10. **Relying**—Believing that the only person you can ever count on is yourself.

11. **Charming**—Believing that other people will never act in your interest unless you first charm and manipulate them.

12. **Name-calling**—Inflicting global names, labels and stereotypes on people which may contain a morsel of truth but are based only on a single observation or incident.

13. **Defaulting**—Feeling helpless because you believe other people and circumstances have control over what you can and cannot do.

14. **Overgeneralizing**—Forcing *big* conclusions from little observations.

15. **Personalizing**—Believing that everything that occurs is related significantly to *you*.

continues

> ### 17 Mindbenders *continued*
>
> 16. **Controlling**—Assuming you have omnipotent power and control, and that you are responsible for everything and everybody.
>
> 17. **Polarizing**—Seeing everything that happens in either/or extremes.

The Fear of Self-Promotion: Call Reluctance

Call reluctance occurs when goal-disruptive feelings accompany distorted perceptions of prospecting. These distortions can occur when perceptions are processed by your past experience, present needs and valuing filters. But be careful. The story does not end there. Your *feelings* are not the problem. They only serve as messengers to alert you to the presence of a problem which has been *created* by your filters.

Your feelings are *always in exact proportion to their actual cause.* In the case of call reluctance, feelings become suspect because they are always found at the scene. There, they become innocent victims of circumstantial evidence and mistaken identity while the actual guilty party remains free to strike again.

Your filters exert their influence through mind chatter, the ongoing process of describing the world to yourself. You continuously carry on an internal dialogue about what you *think* you see and hear. Since this dialogue is a by-product of your filters, its appraisal of a particular prospecting situation is highly subjective. Prospecting situations do not contain meaning in and of themselves. You appraise prospecting outcomes as good or bad, painful or pleasant. You predict whether your next prospecting efforts will be emotionally dangerous or emotionally safe. Then, based on your conclusions, positive emotions move you towards prospecting activities, while negative emotions prepare you to avoid a danger you told yourself lies ahead.

THE ROLE OF SELF-TALK

The labels you pin on things and the judgments you make about them are fashioned from an unending dialogue you have with yourself. Albert Ellis, whose psychotherapeutic model is based on changing behavior by changing internal dialogue, calls your internal chatter "self-talk." Aaron Beck has had an equal impact on the practice of psychotherapy. He calls internal dialogue "automatic thought."

Our work at the Call Reluctance Center has been focused upon the fear of self-promotion. While working in this narrow field, we have chosen the label "self-pressurization" to describe the mental chatter associated with call reluctance.

Charity Begins at Home

We talk to other people differently than we talk to ourselves. We are usually more sensitive, kind, honest, generous and attentive when we converse with others. When we talk to ourselves, privately, about the world as we see it, we often get tangled up in petty childlike habits of thought and emotion. Without realizing it, we color some of the meanings a deep blood-red. In the case of call reluctance, neutral prospects, things and circumstances are inflicted with the residue of our childish fears, adolescent demands for attention and approval, and insistence upon perfect performance in *everything* we do *all* the time. Here's an actual example.

A Career Can Hold Only So Much Pressure

One high-producing computer salesman for a very well-known computer hardware firm attended a Call Reluctance Center workshop a few years ago with a growing dread of prospecting. He was the company's number one salesman, yet the better he got, the more distressed he became when he tried to prospect. He coped successfully by himself for a number of years because he did not know what else to do. His sales managers were too busy maintaining the company's first-rate reputation as a sales organization to be perceptive enough to know that behind their best producer's bravado was a growing, festering, unresolved problem— call reluctance. After a few years of peak performance, his production began to show dangerous signs before inevitably tapering off. He began recycling his business by reselling his current clients. He was not developing new sources of sales. The competition, a younger, leaner, more agile company, was.

"What nobody ever knew," he told other salespeople at the Center, "was the horrifying things I was telling myself about prospecting from the very beginning. Things I never realized like, 'If I don't get more appointments than *anybody else* tonight, then I won't be the *best* . . . and if I'm not the *best*, then I'm a *failure* . . . and if I'm a *failure*, then I can't provide for my family . . . and if I don't provide for my family, people will *ridicule* me . . . and if people *ridiculed* me, *I couldn't stand it.*' "

This salesman enjoyed pointing out two things about his struggle with call reluctance to other salespeople who were presently struggling with the problem. First, the things he was telling himself were *not true*. Second, they had *absolutely nothing to do with prospecting*. His distress was the result of daily doses of self-inflicted verbal poison. But no matter how reckless his self-statements might have been, he *accepted* them as true at the time he said them to himself. He then *acted* as if they were true by always being alert to fictional prospecting dangers and being prepared to do battle with the evil Mr. Prospect. Since coping took energy away from meaningful performance, and Mr. Prospect was never the problem in the first place, the real problem got worse, not better. After a while, he found himself lost in the middle of his career and almost out of gas.

What you say to yourself about prospecting has a powerful impact upon what you feel when prospecting. What you feel when prospecting has a powerful impact on what you do about prospecting.

PULLING THE PLUG
ON CAREER-LIMITING SELF-TALK

How can you find out if *your* self-talk is prospecting poison? If you find that it is, what can you do about it? Other salespeople, veteran and neophyte alike, have found that they can regain control over their emotional response to prospecting by learning four simple steps: 1) Slow Down, 2) Listen In, 3) Replace, and 4) Apply. Let's pause for an overview of each step before starting through the entire Thought Realignment procedure.

First: Slow Down

The insults and offenses you hurl at yourself only need an instant to do their work. Before you can hear the poison-tipped words and phrases, and see the horrible visual images which attend them, you must first slow them down.

If you're like the authors, you get annoyed with self-help experts who say you can move a mountain, but fail to tell you where to get mountain-moving equipment. It is not unusual for a self-help program to advise you to slow down. *But how?*

You can slow down the rate of your internal dialogue by a simple procedure we use at the Call Reluctance Center called *Thought-Deceleration.* Here's how it works.

First, just *talk to yourself.* Don't talk out loud. Talk the way you normally do when you talk to yourself. Then *listen.* Notice how your imaginary voice sounds, then answer the following questions. How loud is it? What is the tone like? How would other people describe your internal voice if they could hear it? If you have trouble hearing your voice, just pretend you hear it, but answer the questions. Perhaps when you read, you sub-vocalize (actually say the words to yourself that you are reading). If so, then use your "reading" voice.

Second, continue to talk to yourself, but purposefully *lower your voice one octave.* Imagine your voice is coming from deep down inside your chest when you talk. Again, if you have trouble, just *pretend* to lower your voice. Three things should now happen. The *pace* of your self-talk automatically slows down when you lower your voice. Your imaginary voice *pronounces* things more clearly. And it becomes easier to *hear* the words and phrases, and *see* the pictures you associate with them.

Here's a third, optional step. Whenever you thought-decelerate, lightly *bite your tongue* and say *out loud*: "This is my thought-deceleration cue. Whenever and wherever I do this I will immediately slow down the pace of my self-talk."

What you have just learned is an automatic method for slowing down the pace of internal self-talk. If you will practice it for five minutes, three times a day for three days, something even more interesting will happen. By just lightly biting your tongue, you will start speaking to yourself in a slower, clearer, more manageable pace. Slowing down enough to take a census of the messages bouncing around inside your head is the first step to cleaning house.

Second: Listen In

Now that you have slowed things down, you can start listening for content. Most of what you see and hear will be about as absorbing as Saturday morning cartoons. But if you are call reluctant, the next time you are prospecting (or about to prospect), turn down the pace and listen in. Soon you will hear your Self-Propaganda Channel broadcasting daily career-busting messages at full strength. Pay attention. You will be introduced to the phantoms that lie beneath the surface of your call reluctance.

Nine Career-Damaging Themes

The things you say to yourself which inhibit your ability to prospect will, if left unchallenged, result in one or more of the nine known types of the fear of self-promotion already described. We have listed below the most common self-talk themes associated with each of the nine types.

Threat Sensitivity

"I *must always* be vigilant and careful to avoid *anything* the least bit fearful or unpredictable."

Desurgency

"I *must always be perfectly* prepared *before* I have the right to initiate contact with any prospective buyer."

Protension

"All managers, colleagues, prospects and clients must see me as thoroughly competent, capable, intelligent and achieving in every respect."

Groups

"In order to be an effective speaker, I must absolutely dazzle everyone in the room with my charm, wit and mastery of the subject."

Friends

"I must *never* do *anything* which would *ever* lead *any* of my friends to think I was trying to exploit them."

Role Acceptance

"*All* salespeople are *just* peddlers, and since I am in sales, *all* the people who expected me to aspire to a dignified occupation *must* be *thoroughly* disappointed."

Disruption Sensitivity

"I *must always* place the interests of other people ahead of my own; and I *must never* interfere or intrude upon them for *any* reason."

Social Differential

"*All* wealthy, educated, positioned people are better than me. I *must always* remember to keep my place and *never* presume to be their equal."

Family

"I *must never* seek to advise *any* member of my own family in any business matters because it is *always* unethical and they will *never* take me seriously anyway."

The Play-By-Play Approach

Sometimes slowing down is not enough to allow you to survey the impact that negative self-talk has on your prospecting. When it's not, try this thought experiment:

Recall an actual prospecting situation which is particularly difficult for you. Now imagine you are listening to a sportscaster's play-by-play description of the things you are saying to yourself while watching the accompanying visual images on the screen of an imaginary television set. When the sportscaster describes a careless thought or reckless bit of self-talk that you would like to observe more closely, request an *instant replay*. Back the scene up several frames. Then let it move forward slowly, frame-by-frame. Give the sportscaster editorial freedom to elaborate on what you are saying to yourself. Zoom in on the pictures you see on the screen. Move in as close as you can. Look at the pictures. Listen to what your sportscaster has to say.

Gil T, a stockbroker from Connecticut, had trouble slowing things down. Thought-deceleration worked but it did not slow things down enough. So he let Howard Cosell help by providing the play-by-play. It worked. Here is how he did it:

> *"Here comes Gil T, a talented newcomer who is not play-ing at his potential. There he goes reaching for the phone. His determination shows, but here comes the old habits back again. Look at his forehead perspire! Listen to what he is saying to himself: "Getting real scared . . . don't know why . . . can't use the phone . . . too scared." Look at that man squirm in his chair! This has happened before folks. He starts to fidget and perspire every time he starts to use the phone; then he starts to tell himself how scared he is."*

Gil soon learned that whenever he reached for the phone he was *telling himself* how scared he was. Simultaneously, he was calling up a mental snapshot of himself *looking panicked*. Then he perspired. Fidgeted. Within seconds he *panicked*. He actually heard himself saying, "I'm *scared. Can't* dial the phone because something *bad* will happen to me. I have *got* to stay away from things that scare me, because if I don't, I'll get hurt. People would see how weak I am and *nobody* will like me because I'm a weakling who's always getting hurt."

Gil learned much about what he was telling himself about prospecting (in his case about using the phone to prospect). Once he slowed things down enough to get in touch with what was happening, he was able to see what he was doing to himself. He could even remember the first time he said those things and had those feelings.

According to Gil, it all began one day at school when he was 11 years old. Ever since, he has been vigilantly trying to avoid "peril" as seen through the eyes of an *11-year-old* version of himself. Eleven-year-old Gil was doing one hell of a job protecting the adult Gil from his childhood fears. But Gil's prospecting activity was in shambles.

Third: Replace

The fear of self-promotion occurs when we allow ourselves to mindlessly recite career-limiting messages and experience the distressful feelings they produce. Thus, the next step is to disconnect the career-limiting thought from the distressing fear it automatically produces. How? By thoughtfully replacing career-limiting chatter with goal-supporting self-statements. Here's a brief exercise which illustrates the logic behind the strategy.

Before you next use the phone to prospect, recite the following statement three times: "I *must* make *everybody* like me or I am nothing." How does reciting this statement influence how you perceive the phone? How does it influence the way you *feel* about using the phone to prospect?

Feelings are an important part of our survival instincts. They do not like being placed in situations which could result in annihilation. Annihilation? Who said anything about annihilation? You did. That is exactly how your feelings interpret the situation when you say " . . . or I am nothing." The only information your feelings have about the up-coming situation is: 1) You are about to use the phone to call people who may not appreciate being called. 2) You *must* make everybody like you. 3) If anyone does not like or approve of you, you will cease to exist. 4) Therefore, you are about to place yourself in a situation which threatens your *very survival*. What fun.

So how do you change this scenario? You replace your fear-producing self-statement with a *non*-fear-producing self-statement.

To illustrate, let's return to the career-limiting self-statement you recited before using the phone. Imagine you are in the exact same prospecting situation. You are about to use the telephone. However, this time recite the following amended version of the previous self-statement three times: "I would *like* to be liked by everyone, because I enjoy being liked for a lot of good reasons." Consider how you feel now as you reach for the phone. Notice the difference in the role your feelings play. In the first example, they were told a potential disaster might occur if you dialed the phone. In the current example, you substituted a *preference* for a nonverifiable requirement. The first version rang an alarm. The second did not because none was needed. The first statement was fear-soliciting, the second was not because there was nothing to fear. One projected the threat of annihilation, the other projected an opportunity. Of the two, which statement is more true? Which is goal-supporting? Which takes more energy?

Fourth: Apply

Thought Realignment would fall short of the mark if all it did was to help you know yourself better or to feel better about yourself. These are commendable goals, but better left to the pep-talkers on motivational cassettes. Insight is not our primary objective. Increased prospecting is.

In keeping with that aim, the next step in Thought Realignment is to *translate what you learn into more phone calls and more seen calls.* For example, if you fear calling on educated professional people, and then act out your fear by not making those calls (or not calling on them often enough in relation to your market), then your action objective is to *initiate contact with more educated people more often.*

Thought Realignment: A Permanent Solution

How does Thought Realignment differ from attitude-changing sermons you can hear on cassettes or in a one-hour pep-talk by Mr. A. Dynamic Motivator? Consider the following differences:

1. The *objectives are different*. This method is designed to help you acquire new and better control of your emotions, particularly those that interfere with prospecting.

2. It is a *system*, and draws from an integrated set of procedures, each of which contributes to the overall objective.

3. The *time-frame* is different. This approach teaches a discipline. It takes time, practice and attention. It is not an entertainment.

4. Applied correctly, Thought Realignment has proven to be more *lasting and durable* than inspirational quick-fixes. If you are a typical salesperson, you may tend to experience *cyclic feelings*. Early in the day, you may be high, expecting nothing but more highs only to find that at the end of the day you are down, expecting nothing but more downs. Inspirational speakers are masters at exploiting this situation. After a few hours of podium-pounding, they get salespeople who are on a high to be momentarily higher, and salespeople who are on a low to think they are high for an hour. But the effect doesn't last for either group, and often damages both.

Don't Blame Your Feelings!

Some ill-fated approaches to managing call reluctance are too centered on feelings of fear. But how you *feel* is not the total problem. Your feelings are just one of the *symptoms* of the problem, the other being insufficient prospecting.

The real culprit is mismanaged emotional energy. Think about it. If every time you have the opportunity to initiate contact with a prospective buyer you silently shout to yourself, "RED ALERT! . . . DANGER AHEAD! . . . ESCAPE IMMEDIATELY!" what do you expect to experience? Feelings of peace? Joy? Serenity?

Feelings are not thoughts. They do not evaluate or discern, they mobilize you to action. Think of them as your obedient servants down in the engine room who follow, without question or argument, whatever instruction you, the pilot, issue. If you have the nasty habit of telling them to prepare for a life-threatening emergency every time you reach for the phone, open the door to your prospect's office, or greet your prospect' receptionist, then *you can be assured that your feelings will respond to the alert by preparing your body to survive a life-threatening emergency.*

So, while it may appear that your feelings have gone berserk, do not jump to conclusions. Do not rush to blame your feelings for doing what they are supposed to be doing. And do not let *other people* play mind games with your emotions.

Some would-be hypnotic games, for example, try to put a quick fix on call reluctance. They try to get you to delude yourself into thinking that you are not feeling fear in situations when you *are* feeling fear. This approach may be harmless in some situations, but in the case of call reluctance, it compounds the problem into one that is much more difficult to deal with for everyone concerned. Be careful!

Positive mental attitude games, on the other hand, do not try to hypnotize you. Instead, they attempt to get you to *deny* your feelings. That could be helpful in some situations, but in the case of call reluctance, it could be psychically brutal and extremely damaging. Be careful!

Don't get seduced by drug games with lightning fast prescription pens. Valium and other mood anesthetics can cause problems far more severe than an honest dose of call reluctance. And that goes for alcohol and other consumer chemicals. They might anesthetize painful feelings, but they never offer a solution to the problem. Be careful!

PART TWO

THOUGHT REALIGNMENT STEP-BY-STEP

Up to now you have surveyed the basics of Thought Realignment. But how can you apply it to your day-to-day prospecting activities? Thought Realignment has been popular at the Call Reluctance Center because it consists of well-defined steps which are interesting and easy to learn. Salespeople who have used this procedure have seen significant and lasting improvements in record time. But how much and how soon you benefit from Thought Realignment depends upon which *type* of call reluctance you have, how long you have had it, and whether you have been victimized by ill-advised quick fixes which may have strengthened the habits you are now trying to break.

STEP ONE
GENERAL FEELING CONSEQUENCES I (GFC's)

Take out a piece of paper and write down a list of words which, in your judgment, describe what call reluctance feels like. Title your list "GFC's" for General Feeling Consequences. ACTION BREAK

The feeling consequences you just listed are some of the ways that call reluctance signals its presence. These signals work the same as warning lights on the dashboard of your car. Their job is to *signal* the presence of a problem. They themselves are not the problem.

The Difference Between Label and Content

In today's over-psychologized society, we are losing the ability to accurately describe our own problems in terms we can meaningfully deal with. We constantly get sidestepped into using fashionable scientific names to describe our distress. Then when we attempt to do something about our problem, we find that the names evaporate into words without substance.

Let's look closer by taking a brief mind trip. Imagine you are standing naked in the middle of a snowstorm. Got it? Now Pause. Take a few seconds and try to describe what is happening. Then take out a piece of paper and write down your observations as accurately as you can. ACTION BREAK.

Most salespeople who have taken this curious trip say things like, "I get cold." Some say, "I'm uncomfortable." At least one always says,

"I'm embarrassed." Occasionally, there is an individual who is unable or unwilling to fantasize the situation at all.

Consider this. When you say you are *cold*, you are correct in the *figurative sense*. But that is not particularly instructive. Cold is not what is happening to you. Cold is the label you *attach* to the variety of sensations you are experiencing.

Let's look at it from another perspective. Imagine you are at a convenience store to buy a bottle of ketchup. You place your order with the clerk. He reaches up and grabs a bottle with a label that reads "ketchup." So far, so good. That's what you wanted. But then he takes a razor from a nearby drawer and scrapes off the label. He hands you the label and says, "That will be $1.25 please." You do not let the situation pass uncontested. You demand the *contents* of the bottle. That's what you thought you were paying for and that's what you believe you are entitled to. And so you are.

Now return to the snowstorm. You are still standing there naked. But this time when you are asked what is happening, instead of just saying you are cold, ask yourself what cold stands for. Demand *the contents*. What *exactly* is happening to you that causes you to assign the label "cold?"

By this time, most salespeople say, "Well, I'm turning blue!" Others say, "I've got goose bumps all over." Still others point out, "I'm shivering!" Interestingly enough, what one individual calls cold may not be what another experiences as cold.

The MAD Test

When you check out a label, use the MAD test. MAD is an acronym which stands for "Make Any Difference?" Does it make any difference to use this word or that label to describe what is happening? Does it point you in a helpful direction? Does it provide a solution? Does it provide meaningful guidance? Labels like "stress," "primary call reluctance," "secondary call reluctance," and the time-worn "fear-of-rejection" are word games. They sound sophisticated but fail the MAD test. They do not reveal, direct, change, enlighten or instruct in any way that *makes a difference*. Listen to the following advice taken from an insurance industry publication:

"Sales anxiety (*a label for what?*) is a normal occurrence in this business, but too often the occasional day or two of call reluctance turns into weeks and months of poor production. When the early symptoms are ignored, the problem can have a snowball effect: fear of failure (*another label!*) can cause poor performance, resulting in greater fear of failure (*still another label!*) causing worse performance . . ."

The next time a consultant tells you that your sales career is burdened down by the "fear-of-rejection," apply the MAD test. Ask if that information alone is suppose to cure you, or if something more instructive is going to follow.

Descriptors like "goose bumps," 'turning blue," and "shivering" can be verified by *observation*. They are your body's mode of communicating to you that your temperature is lowering to potentially dangerous levels and that you need to seek warmth. Note that you would not die from exposure to the cold immediately. There are hints, signs and symptoms all along the way. What are they? "Goose bumps," "turning blue," and "shivering." Notice that in our example, shivering serves two purposes. First, it signals that something is amiss. Second, by starting your body in motion, it directs you to get moving.

The Case of Positive Paul

Some salespeople, like Positive Paul, do not accept information on this level. They are perpetually tuned in to top-40's pop psych chit-chat and will not listen to anything that does not ring of modern mental mysticism. With an ear full of confusing jargon, they ignore their bodys' simple but elegant way of informing them that something needs serious attention *now*.

Standing there naked in the middle of a snowstorm, Positive Paul is turning blue. He has goose bumps and is freezing to death. So what does Positive Paul do? He tells himself, "I won't let a little cold weather get me down. I'll put on Dr. Moonbeam's exciting new *Positive Brainpower* tape."

After a few minutes, Positive Paul looks positively bizarre. There he is standing naked in the middle of a snowstorm, with a frozen grin, trying to convince himself that he is soaking up sunshine on the warm, sunny beaches of Hawaii.

A Matter of Priorities

If you were driving down the street and your oil pressure gauge glowed a bright red, what would you do? Most people would take that as a sign to *immediately* pull the vehicle over and check the problem. They would not complain about the color, and they certainly would not try to pretend that it was a bright *green*.

Would you ignore the signal and keep on driving? Would you pat your car on the dashboard and reassuringly say, "You must be upset. We don't need a negative attitude here, now do we? So let's listen to Dr. Moonbeam's new motivational cassette, *Turning Panic into Profit*."

If you are like most people, you would not treat your car that way.

You should not treat yourself that way either. When you are prospecting and your "warning lights" glow bright red, pull over, lift the hood, and take an honest look.

The Experience of Call Reluctance Revisited

So far, two things have been clarified. First, we cleaned up our understanding of what the actual experience of call reluctance feels like from the perspective of sensations. Second, we found out how salespeople and their managers spend their energy and money chasing after, and trying to correct, *labels* for call reluctance *instead of the problem itself.*

STEP TWO
GENERAL FEELING CONSEQUENCES II (GFC's)

Take out another sheet of paper and try again to list what you think call reluctance feels like. *But this time no labels, just content.* Title your chart GFC's II for General Feeling Consequences, version two. Concentrate on what actually happens, what is being *experienced.* Remember, if you can't think of anything, just pretend, but *do the exercise.* Here's an example to help you get started. It is a list of three things call reluctance actually felt like to the authors.

Heart pounding

Dry mouth

Nervous stomach

Now it's your turn. ACTION BREAK.

Inventory Of Call Reluctance Experiences

How did you do? Did you permit labels to infiltrate your list? Here are some of the most common experiences other salespeople have listed through the years.

Sensations Reported	Percent Experiencing
Butterflies in stomach	28%
Perspiring more than usual	34%
Fidget, can't keep still	7%
Breath faster, shallower	10%

Hyperventilation	2%
Get very thirsty	3%
Have to go to the bathroom often	16%
Cry	1%
Heart pounding	42%
Voice rises to higher pitch	13%
Mind goes blank	7%
Get the shakes	6%
Stammer and stutter	18%
Talk louder and/or faster	43%
Pupils dilate	5%
Chest feels tight	21%

Total does not equal 100% due to some respondents reporting multiple sensations.

When call reluctance is examined from the perspective of what is actually *happening*, it can be seen for what it is, a serious, energy-sapping parasite. Labels like "fear of rejection" or "fear of success" are more sophisticated and respectable than admitting that you have to go to the bathroom whenever you try to prospect, or stammer every time you initiate contact with a prospective buyer.

Signs of distress, like those inventoried above, *are the problem.* They keep you from devoting full energy to prospecting. They will remain the problem, regardless of the label you attach, until you can reach for the phone without showing signs of distress. The battle lines are drawn.

STEP THREE
PERSONAL FEELING CONSEQUENCES (PFC's)

Take out another piece of paper and compile your own personal inventory of call reluctance experiences. Begin by referring to the last list you constructed (GFC's II) and the Inventory of Call Reluctance Experiences we provided. List all sensations *you yourself actually feel when you try to prospect.* Be sure to include all the experiences you feel even if they do not appear on the other two lists. Watch out for labels! ACTION BREAK.

STEP FOUR
GENERAL ACTIVATING EVENTS (GAE's)

So far, you have listed *specific* "feeling consequences" of call reluctance *for salespeople in general*. You then made a *personal* list of what call reluctance feels like to you. Now we will proceed one step closer to the origin of call reluctant feelings. You do not feel your "PFC's" *everywhere* or *all the time*. So, the next step is to identify *when* you do experience them and under *what* conditions.

Take out another piece of paper. Set it up as shown in the example below. Then, based on your experience and knowledge of prospecting in general, list as many call reluctance "where's" and "what's" as you can. If you don't know any, or can't think of any, then just *pretend, but do the exercise.*

Where	What
When I'm sitting at my desk	getting ready to cold call.
(*Where* I am)	(Exactly *what* I am doing)

Now it's your turn. ACTION BREAK.

How many different situations did you list? Persons attending classes at the Call Reluctance Center usually come up with long and enlightening lists. Let's see how yours compares to theirs. Here is an example of some of the more common situations listed by them over the years.

- "When I realize that it is about time to ask for a referral."
- "When I look at my watch and notice that in about five minutes I'm supposed to be using the phone to prospect."
- "When I am driving in my car and pull up in the parking lot for my first call on someone."
- "When I get to the building and see my prospect's name, title or educational degrees on the building directory."
- "When I am about to place a prospecting call on the phone and notice that I only have a few prospect cards left and wonder where my next ones will come from."
- "When I dial the phone and a secretary answers."
- "When I dial the phone and the prospect answers."

- "When I get right outside the door of my prospect's office and reach to open it."
- "When I'm in the waiting room mentally rehearsing what I'm going to say."

Are you familiar with any of these situations? We call them GAE's for General Activating Events. They may be familiar to you, but as you can see, they are by no means *unique* to you.

STEP FIVE
PERSONAL ACTIVATING EVENTS (PAE's)

Review the list you have just constructed. Then take out another piece of paper. Set it up the same as you did in Step Four. This time, however, list only those situations which *apply specifically to you*. These will be your PAE's for Personal Activating Events. Be certain to include on your list any that are applicable to you even if they did not appear in your general list or the list we provided. ACTION BREAK.

STEP SIX
PUTTING IT TOGETHER

Now let's consolidate what we have learned so far. Set up a new piece of paper like the example below. Then, under the first column, copy your Personal Activating Events (PAE's)." Under the second column, copy the specific emotional reactions you listed on the other form you completed called Personal Inventory of Call Reluctance Experiences (PFC's II). ACTION BREAK.

Where I Am/What I'm Doing	My Emotional Reaction
(PAE's)	(PFC's)
"Prospect answers phone"	"My mind goes blank"
"Arrive at prospect's office"	"Heart starts pounding"

How did you do? Were you able to bring into sharper focus *exactly what feelings you have in specific prospecting situations*?

For some salespeople, the problem seems to become more manageable once they are able to break it down, diagram and plot it out.

The scale becomes smaller. The problem consists of more clearly definable components.

Now our job must be directed to the next step, the search for the missing link which connects your PAE's to your PFC's. In other words, we now begin searching for the wires which connect your feelings to the prospecting situation.

STEP SEVEN
THE SEARCH FOR THE MISSING LINK

If you are like most salespeople, trainers, consultants and managers, your last exercise resulted in a mirage. It appears that what you *feel* (PFC's) is connected to where you are and what you are *doing* (PAE's). That inference is lethal. To accept it as is actually *causes* call reluctance and *maintains* it once it occurs.

Since it appears that the prospect's voice on the other end of the phone is what *makes* my mind go blank, I incorrectly conclude that *if I stop or reduce my telephone prospecting, then my mind will not go blank.* Since it appears that my tight stomach is caused by my arrival at the prospect's office, I wrongly conclude that *if I do not go to his office, or go to the address but don't actually enter the building (null calls), then my stomach will not be tight.*

Many well-intended but seriously flawed solutions for call reluctance are based upon the presumption that the *setting* is somehow linked to your emotional *reactions.* But take a closer look at the consolidation exercise (Step Six) you just completed. Your reactions are physically real. They are *not* imaginations. They exert a very *real*, negative pressure on your ability to prospect. But is there an *actual* connection between them and prospecting? Are there any *wires* that connect your head to the telephone which explain the negative shock you get whenever you try to dial? The answer is no.

The presumption that where we are (PAE's) *causes* what we *feel* (PFC's) is part of the *problem*, not the solution. Misleading explanations which reinforce the fictional connection between the two tend only to *strengthen* the problem. They do not reduce it. Furthermore, if events (PAE's) *did* cause feelings (PFC's), then our prospects *actually could* terrorize us and we would have an *objective* reason to fear them. But in most cases, prospects are feared *before* they are met.

The following is an actual example of misleading advice which subtly presumes that prospecting events (PAE's) are the cause of goal-disruptive feelings (PFC's). Uncritical acceptance of advice like this can lead to compounding an already existing problem.

"The primary way to cope with call reluctance is to experience a series of successful calls, and the key to that end is to remain active."

"To Sidestep Rejection . . . we phone for appointments. But we are different here (than other insurance agencies) in that we identify ourselves as financial planners, not insurance agents."

Using the MAD test as a barometer, let's examine the above statements more closely. According to the MAD test, when you isolate the real cause, you should be able to do three things. First, you should be able to prove that every salesperson who has been exposed to the toxin should be sick. In other words, every salesperson who experiences a series of unsuccessful sales calls should develop call reluctance. Secondly, they should be sickened in direct proportion to their *degree* of exposure. The greater the exposure, the greater the severity of the symptoms you should observe. Third, you should be able to find a toxin that, when removed, *causes the symptoms to disappear.*

The advice in the first quote is based upon the presumption that unsuccessful calls mysteriously make a salesperson call reluctant. But does *every* salesperson become call reluctant after one unsuccessful sales call? If it takes more than one unsuccessful call, then exactly *how* many are required? Two? Three? Five? Ten? If only *some* salespeople become call reluctant after one or more unsuccessful calls, then do they become reluctant to the *exact same degree*? If not, why not?

The second bit of advice presumes that the *role* of an insurance agent inherently *causes* call reluctance. But does it? Do *all* insurance agents have call reluctance? Since the quote presumes that it originates from a single common source, just *being* an insurance agent, then do agents who have call reluctance have it to the *exact same degree*? Of course not. The real cause is yet to be discovered.

Private Meanings Revisited

An intermediate step exists between the instant we assign meaning to an experience and our emotional reaction to that meaning. So far, we have referred to this step as "self-talk."

Experience does not come to us prepackaged. It comes in the form of raw, unprocessed data. How we process the data of our experience varies with each individual. During processing, we assign meaning to our life experiences. We then react to the assigned meaning, not to the experience itself.

There are two basic types of meanings which can be generated from our self-talk: self-*enhancing* and self-*diminishing*. Self-enhancing self-talk is more consistent with the actual data of our experience and results in *appropriate* emotional responses. It has the following general characteristics:

1. It is *flexible*.

2. It permits an *offensive* response to problems.

3. It helps you feel *in control*.

4. It allows you to consider *options*.

Self-diminishing self-talk, however, is different. It explodes and amplifies emotional responses beyond the level required by the actual data of the experience. It inflicts unnecessary feelings which are unmanageable and overwhelming. Its general characteristics are:

1. It *rigidly* results in the same reaction regardless of the situation.

2. It is *defensive*.

3. It *takes control*. You just go along for the ride.

4. It implies that you have *no options*.

You can easily spot self-diminishing self-talk by simply observing what it does to your prospecting behavior. Intense feelings are aroused when they are not wanted or needed. Self-pressurizing words invade your mental vocabulary. Once there, they distort your running narration of the prospecting situation and steal energy which would have been allocated to support your prospecting objectives. Here are a few examples:

Instead of saying . . .
"*I would like to* land three sales appointments,"
you say . . .
"*I have to* land three sales appointments, *or else*."

Instead of saying . . .
"*I would prefer* to be the best sales prospector around,"
you say . . .
"*I must be* the best sales prospector around, *or else*."

Self-Inflicted Ghosts and Goblins

The authors often have the opportunity to speak before large and influential audiences. We know that if we do well in these presentations, several large sales could result. Assuming we are motivated and our motivation is focused on the presentation, what goal-supporting behaviors should be expected?

- Would we prepare?

- How would we handle questions?

- What would be our attitude towards the people in the audience?

On the other hand, what would happen if we constantly told ourselves that we *had* to deliver the very best presentation those people ever heard?

- The intensity of our emotions would probably *interfere* with our ability to prepare.

- We would probably *act* like we were experts in *everything*.

- We would relate rigidly to the audience.

- We would *blame* the intensity of our feelings on the audience and call it "stage fright."

But wait. Was it the *audience* that caused our stage fright? Did they find a way to *cause* us to experience counter-productive feelings? Or was it something we did to ourselves as we interpreted the situation we found ourselves in?

We intended to tell ourselves to prepare for an opportunity which could move us closer to our goals. Instead, we wound up saying that it was *imperative* (not just desirable) to do a good job, that we *had* to dazzle *everybody* there (an impossible task), and then we implied that if we failed to do these things, something *absolutely horrible* would happen (which would not). So instead of performing well, we had to cope with self-inflicted ghosts and goblins which we projected onto the audience.

Some Good Reasons for Talking Straight to Yourself

There are several techniques you can use to distinguish goal-supporting self-talk from the twisted, contorted and limiting self-talk we have described. Here are a few.

Goal-supporting self-talk is . . .

1. VERIFIABLE. It should be obvious why anybody prefers to perform well as opposed to poorly. On the other hand, the belief that you *must* perform well is totally *unverifiable*. Test it out. You will find several good reasons to support the case for good performance. But these reasons only serve to further illustrate why you *desire* certain outcomes, not why you *must have them*.

2. LOGICALLY CONSISTENT. It moves you *closer* to, not further away from, the things you want.

3. UPLIFTING. It permits you to have more pleasant feelings more often.

4. OBJECTIVE. It helps you to form more accurate assessments of situations, choose from among available alternatives, and realistically estimate the probable consequences of your actions.

5. LIBERATING. It contributes to the *solution* of problems, not the strengthening or continuation of them.

6. EDUCATIONAL. It allows you to learn from your good and bad experiences, reducing the likelihood that the same problems will reoccur.

When these criteria are applied to internal dialogue, it becomes apparent that some of the things you are saying to yourself are *not* goal-supporting. They are goal-*obstructing*.

Altered States

Can you think of a song that brings to mind the face of a special person? Is there a perfume or an after-shave that automatically invokes the memory of a special past experience? Certain cues, like a particular piece of music, a certain smell, a touch, a vague internal sensation, or even certain words, can cause you to vividly *reexperience* highly charged past experiences. *Career-damaging self-talk* works the same way. A cue which has become associated with a distressful event from the past starts the wheels in motion. We then *relive* the experience as if it were happening again, now.

Cues can also be embedded in prospecting situations. When prospecting, some salespeople actually go into an altered state of consciousness and for a moment become oblivious to what is going on around them. Has that ever happened to you? If so, you could be *hypnotizing yourself into call reluctance every time you process a particular cue.*

One salesperson told the authors how she experienced distressful feelings associated with prospecting whenever she saw a computer print-out. It seems that her first and last day in magazine subscription sales was particularly traumatic. She was seated in a booth with a phone, a sales script and a huge computer list of names and telephone numbers. She started out high on confidence but low on training and mental preparation. It didn't take more than a couple of hours for the printout to become indelibly associated with feelings of despair and distress. The telephone ceased to be an instrument of opportunity and instead became associated with unpleasant sensations. Even the blue color of her cubicle took on a negative imprint. Now, whenever she sees a computer print-out, an office telephone or a blue cubicle, she remembers her experience and *relives how she felt.*

The Negative Power of Words

Negative self-talk consists of *highly charged word cues* which can *cut* and *hurt*. When used, these words will automatically invoke sensations associated with distressful past experiences. Words which typically work in this way include, "it would be *terrible*," "*awful*," "*horrible*," "*couldn't stand it*," "*tragedy*," and "*catastrophe* if." Sometimes a single, incidental event in the course of sales training can be enough to set the process in motion.

During her training as a chemical salesperson, Barbara T was insensitively corrected *in front of her prospect* by her young sales trainer. Following a minor error in her presentation, she remembers him smiling condescendingly and pointing out to her prospect that she was "new in the business." Following that incident, whenever she saw *anyone* smile at her in the same manner and ask, "How long have you been in the business?" she *replayed the earlier event*. Her self-talk then took over and *amplified* the situation as follows: "Since this smile is like that smile, *this* person must be like that person, and no person is *ever* going to treat me that way again, *ever*." Prior to attending the Call Reluctance Center, Barbara T had the reputation for being hostile and uncoachable. Bright, young, highly motivated sales trainers reported having the most trouble.

Counterfeit Messages

No matter how peculiar, bizarre or unbelievable it may seem to others, negative self-talk always passes as truth to the salesperson involved. Untested, it has the same truth value as any other source of information, even your immediate sensory experience. For example, whenever Sid G, a financial planner, saw Marty receive a sales performance award, he would automatically launch an internal assault. He would say, "He's got it made. He has a lot of advantages I don't have, and he doesn't care for *anybody but himself*!" To Sid, the conclusions he drew while talking to himself in this way were true. This type of self-propaganda tends to camouflage the real issue. Instead of concentrating on why he was not performing at a level equal to his ability, Sid became preoccupied with the production of other people who were. His self-poisoning thoughts became more real each time they were repeated. And he repeated them every time Marty or anyone else was recognized for outstanding sales performance. Only when Sid learned that his self-talk was not objectively true was he able to see that he was wasting his energy and sacrificing his sales career in the process. Up until that time, he had never tested, verified, challenged or evaluated his internal dialogue, nor had he considered its consequences.

How to Make Prospecting Distressful

- Never try to hear what you are telling yourself that prospecting *means* to you.

- Always *presume* your fears about prospecting are based upon *undisputable fact.*

- When you are distressed by prospecting, always *fix* your attention on how you *feel.* Then trust your feelings to guide you quickly out of the situation and exclude any reasonable information that does not agree with the awful things you are telling yourself.

- Always concentrate on self-limiting themes such as your failures, inabilities, imperfections and lost opportunities. And by all means, dwell incessantly on a bleak outlook for the future.

- Never try to change. If you do, do it half-heartedly.

You were not born with career-damning self-talk. It was acquired in most cases without your even knowing it. Perhaps it was the result of an ill-advised sales training program or a well-intentioned but poorly trained sales manager. Where it came from is not important. The fact that you learned it, however, is very important. With a determined will and the right methods, *you can unlearn it.*

Nine Themes of Traumatic Prospecting

Through the years, the authors have found that the self-talk which interferes with prospecting can be reduced to nine common themes. These themes correspond to the nine known forms of call reluctance. They are listed below.

Threat Sensitivity

"I *must* be *absolutely* careful not to put myself in any danger of any type, because I could *not* handle it and that would be the end of me."

Desurgency

"I *must* be *absolutely* prepared before I initiate *any* contact with prospective buyers, because *any one* of them could ask me a question I couldn't answer. Then they would think I was stupid and superficial and *I could never handle that.*"

How Rational Should You Be?

Should you be gray, pin-striped rational *all* the time? Some adherents of call reluctance approaches similar to Thought Realignment believe you *should*. But is that self-enhancing? We don't think it is. We see this as a self-contradiction. It is not reasonable to be rational *all the time*. The object of Thought Realignment is to help you recover the ability to choose from among various behavioral alternatives, not to replace one form of self-limitation with another, even if the other is based in rationality. We prefer having a *choice*. We want you to be free to act mature or immature, caring or petty, optimistic or depressed, and even call reluctant *if you want to*. We would like for you to have those choices. We do not want you to exchange one set of constraints for another.

Protension

"People *must always* respect me. If they didn't, I wouldn't have any control over them and if I didn't have control over them, I know that I would be *totally vulnerable* and *they would destroy me*."

Groups

"I *must never* screw up in front of a group. If I did, they would *all* think I was incompetent and I know *I could never survive that*."

Friends

"I must *never* call on my friends because one of them might think I was trying to exploit him and *I could never bear the thought* that one of my friends would *ever* think of me that way."

Family

"I could *never* call on my relatives because I *know* they would *never* take me seriously, and if any of them should ever fail to take me seriously *I could not handle it*."

Disruption Sensitivity

"I *must* be loved by *everyone*. I know that if I were to call on people who are not expecting a call, *one* of them might think I was intrusive and *I could never handle that*."

Role

"I *must never* fail to meet the expectations of *other* people, and I *just know* everybody looks upon salespeople as being selfish and dishonest. *I could not handle it* if anyone ever thought that way about me."

Social Differential

"I *know* that I should *never* step out of my place and presume to be good enough to call on people who are better educated or wealthier than I am, because they would quickly discover that I am not as classy as they are and *I could never handle* being reminded of that."

These general themes, when inserted between your prospecting situation (PAE's) and your emotional reaction to that situation (PFC's), fit like the parts of a perfectly formed puzzle. But one theme will fit better than the others. When that theme is discovered, you will have found the real connection between the prospecting situation and why you react to that situation in the way you do.

Once you have reviewed the Nine Themes of Traumatic Prospecting listed previously, take out the last form you completed in Step Six (Putting It Together). As you read through your list, write down the themes that best fit between your Personal Activating Events (PAE's) and your Personal Feeling Consequences (PFC's). Following is an example from the author's experience to get you started.

Where I Am/What I'm Doing (PAE)	My Emotional Reaction (PFC)
About to make a prospecting phone call	Hyperventilating

Self-Talk Theme
(STT)

"I should *never* try to sell *anybody anything*, because that would make me a salesperson and they are self-interested and manipulative—things no one should *ever* think I am."
(Author's version of Role Acceptance theme)

Making a phone call (PAE) does not sufficiently explain the presence of the author's hyperventilation. However, when the self-talk themes were inserted one at a time, one fit better than the others, forming a logical connection between the author's PAE and PFC. Notice that the author was not saying that he did not want people to see him as a pushy or manipulative salesperson. What he was really doing was *demanding* that *nobody ever* see him as being pushy and manipulative. If anyone ever did, he believed it would be *absolutely catastrophic*.

Now it's your turn. ACTION BREAK.

THOUGHT REALIGNMENT IN THE REAL WORLD

"Wow, Mr. Science, now that I know all this, am I *cured*?" No. Call reluctance is not a problem of knowing. It is a problem of *doing*. In order to claim a victory, you must move closer to your real world prospecting goals. You must apply what you have just learned to actual prospecting situations.

Clearing Questions:
Unplugging Performance-Limiting Self-Talk

We always have at least two choices when we are faced with distressful prospecting situations. We can try to change the situation or we can accept it as it is and change how we *feel* about it. In the case of call reluctance, the greatest difficulty is experienced when the situation is unchangeable and we are forced to deal directly with our feelings *about* prospecting.

As you recall from earlier in this chapter, it is imperative that you first identify the alarming things you tell yourself *about* prospecting. Once this is accomplished, you must *interrupt* these self-limiting belief statements and replace them with ones that are goal-supporting. To actively challenge old beliefs and the poisonous self-talk which attends them, you may find it useful to use the following three "clearing" questions.

Clearing Question #1

Whenever you feel a debilitating negative emotion when prospecting, chances are you are reciting a self-pressurizing belief without realizing it. When this happens, *immediately* listen in on your internal dialogue, identify the belief that is detonating your fear response, and *pounce on it*. Begin by asking the first clearing question: "Where's the *proof* that this has to be a *frightening* prospecting situation?" Or you can ask, "Where's the *connection* between my fear in this prospecting situation and what is *supposed* to be scaring me? *Show* it to me!"

The first clearing question, in its various forms, is a direct attack on your *reasoning*. It is a demand for *evidence*. If no convincing evidence is forthcoming, you will have discovered that you can continue to feel fear *if you want to*, but there are no compelling *reasons* for doing so. Blaming the fear on the prospecting situation is *unreasonable*.

Are You Dependent on Cures?

Some salespeople are true believers. They *believe* they can change *only if* they attend an emotionally charged workshop, listen to a melodramatic, motivational cassette, or read a self-help book like this one. For true believers, can the cure *become* part of the problem? Is *your* career being held hostage by books, cassettes and workshops?

Richard A, trust officer at a major northeastern bank, suffered from Desurgent Call Reluctance. He spent far too much time organizing and planning and much too little time prospecting. He learned to identify and control the fear he associated with prospecting by demanding, "What's the *connection*? How can asking me a question I can't answer *cause* me to feel *fear*?" By challenging the belief for evidence, it became apparent to Richard that *no one* could *cause* him to feel *anything* he did not first tell himself to feel. So, what was he telling himself to feel?

Richard traced the real source of his feelings to the *belief* he held that if he *ever* made a mistake, people would not take him seriously, and if people did not take him seriously, it would be *terrible, horrible and catastrophic*. While in an actual prospecting situation, he snagged the belief as it flew by and demanded, "Wait a minute! Where's the *evidence* that I would not be taken seriously if I *ever* made a mistake? *Who* wouldn't take me seriously? Maybe they wouldn't take me seriously *regardless* of whether I made a mistake or not, so why am I holding up my career for *them*?" Being technical and somewhat analytical, all Richard needed was to see the illogic of what he was believing about himself. That was enough for him. He simply shut off the feelings by pulling the self-belief rug out from under them. But for some salespeople one clearing question is not enough.

Clearing Question #2

You may have difficulty snagging these goal-limiting self-belief missiles as they glide by on their destructive paths. So a second clearing question has been positioned to help in these situations: "Do *I have to* feel the *fear* I am feeling right *now* in this prospecting situation? Does the prospecting situation *require* me to feel it?"

If you find yourself saying, "No, the situation cannot really *force* me to feel *this* way," then you have discovered something very important: You have *a choice* about what you *feel* in prospecting situations. *You do* not have to automatically be afraid; therefore, you do not have to act afraid.

If you are like some salespeople, however, the insight that weakens the illusory bond between prospecting fears and actual prospecting situations still remains elusive. Your reply to clearing question number two may be, "Yes, of *course I have to* feel the way I'm feeling. I can tell *you* have never been call reluctant or you wouldn't ask such stupid questions!" So another clearing question is available for a third line of attack.

Clearing Question #3

The first two clearing questions are rational attacks on the *kinds* of feelings you have when you prospect. The third clearing question is an attack on the *degree*: "Even if I believe that I *have to* feel the fear I am feeling (clearing question number one), and that I cannot feel any other way (clearing question number two), then do I have to feel my fear as much as I am feeling it now? Could I amplify it and feel it more if I wanted to? Could I diminish it and feel it less? Do I have to stay *so* upset that I cannot make calls *while* I am feeling this way?"

Newton R, a young sales manager for a midwestern sales training company, was having trouble recruiting new consultant-trainers. His limitation was found to be disruption sensitivity call reluctance. He was not initiating contact with centers-of-influence and other important contacts in his community because he dreaded being intrusive. The first two clearing questions failed to neutralize the beliefs producing the negative self-talk which then neutralized him. So Newt got to the third clearing question and something happened. He found that although he could not easily shake his fear, he could control how *much* fear he felt *while* recruiting. Newton learned that being afraid was not enough to keep him from recruiting. He found the volume control and turned his fear down. That was a legitimate beginning. Soon thereafter he found the on-off switch.

The clearing questions begin the process of pulling the plug on call reluctance. A few salespeople never get that far. They refuse to objectively evaluate and consider the product of their own reasoning. If you are one of them, where does that leave you?

If your answer to *all* the clearing questions is, "Yes, I can *prove* that prospecting scares me, and that I *have to* feel *fear* when I prospect, *and I cannot prospect when I feel fear*," then you have assumed a non-negotiable, flat-world perspective. Based on your beliefs, prospecting will *always* be a fearful, edge-of-the-world experience. Why? Because you accept the *belief* that prospecting *situations* directly *cause* your feelings and even determine how *much* fear you experience.

Dealing With the Source Makes the Difference

Doesn't just forging ahead and making calls despite how you feel just reinforce the old, automatic fear responses? No. By using Thought Realignment you actively sell yourself on the *truth* about the situation *while you are prospecting*. You do this by reminding yourself 1) that there is *no reason* to be afraid, 2) or you can *be* afraid and make calls anyway. Then, you *immediately* put your self-persuasive efforts to work by *acting* as if you are not afraid.

It is the *combination* of first dealing with the *source* of the feeling and then practicing new goal-supporting *behaviors* which separate Thought Realignment from the "just make calls anyway" school of sales management.

The old approach does not deal effectively with the actual *source* of your feelings (self-talk). Therefore, instead of helping, it strengthens the implied connection between making calls and distressful feelings, thus making the problem worse instead of better. Failure to neutralize the underlying beliefs while making calls leads to self-brutalization. It works for a few but it kills as often as it cures. You probably know someone who tried it. You may have tried it yourself. If it and other folk cures actually worked, then call reluctance would not still be the social disease of the direct sales profession.

Remember: **To effectively reduce or eliminate call reluctance, you must precede the right actions with the right thoughts. Do not do one without the other.**

Bernard G, ChFc, CFP, CLU, is a financial planner in the northwest. He has all the right credentials, belongs to all the right organizations, and considers himself a professional among professionals. But he does not have many clients. Bernard *refuses to promote himself.* He considers it unnecessary and unprofessional. Bernard does suspect that something is wrong, but hesitates to call it fear or to ask for help. He completed the Sales Preference Questionnaire (Call Reluctance Test). His scores showed a career-lethal dose of protensive call reluctance. His body showed up at the Call Reluctance Center but his mind held out. He insisted that prospecting does cause "the fear of rejection." In response to the first clearing question, he cited four experts from his industry and played two taped presentations recorded at an annual convention for insurance sales managers. The more we pointed out the logical futility of his position the more defensive he became. The second clearing question did not clear him either. It *confused* him. He could not allow himself to grasp and take responsibility for the feelings he was internally generating when he tried to prospect. The third clearing question produced a monologue of pseudo-psychological jargon which, to the untrained, might have seemed impressive. Bernard's position was fixed and his message was clear. To him the world of prospecting is a hostile and unattractive place. For Bernard, it is destined by his own choice to stay that way. He is his own jailor.

If you agree with Bernard, your unquestioning *belief* in a cause-effect connection between external situations and internal feelings precludes anyone or anything from helping you, so long as you continue to hold, recite and protect this belief. Holding this position places you permanently in a perpetual loop of self-victimization where you will remain and spin until centrifugal force or life trauma frees you from this delusional orbit.

Installing New Prospecting Habits

The clearing questions are the first part of a two part process. They cleared the way for the cultivation of new behaviors which are more consistent with your prospecting goals. The second part of the process is to act consistent with your prospecting goals *while continuously applying the clearing questions.* The combination of active challenging and behavioral defiance can knock out entrenched call reluctant habits which have withstood the efforts of battalions of consultants and trainers alike.

THE PARABLE OF THE NEW ELDORADO

Part 1

The Failure

Imagine for a moment that the authors have persuaded you to believe the following: To convince us that you are a person of worth and ability—a person worth knowing and being with—we first *prefer* to see you driving a new Eldorado and *nothing else*. With this in mind, say to yourself, "In order for Dudley and Goodson to see people as having worth, they always prefer to first see them driving a new Eldorado and nothing else. That means if *I* want them to see *me* as worthwhile and accomplished, then they would prefer to see *me* driving a new Eldorado, too."

It's a mild Tuesday afternoon in your city. It has just rained and you are out driving around on business. You pull up to a red light. There, in the next lane, you see Dudley and Goodson. There we are, waiting for the light to change. We are looking straight through you with a punishing moral squint as you, in an old beat-up Volkswagon bus, wait for the light to change. Looking back at us, as we obviously are looking at you, *how do you feel?* Upset? Small? Insignificant? Depressed?

A Chance To Atone

Being generous and charitable, we condescendingly smile and give you the opportunity to atone for disappointing us. We offer to forgive you *if* you will sign over to us all you now own or ever will own. Furthermore, you must terminate your present job and gain some other employment more to our satisfaction. To us, based on the vehicle you are driving, you would be more suited to late night street cleaning. Do you find this offer acceptable?

Or do you catch yourself saying, "*No way.* I don't feel *that* bad?" Do you become indignant? Do you hear yourself tell us off in no uncertain terms? Do you even feel a little *anger*?

If you do, join in and close ranks. Most salespeople insist, some passionately, that it's *not that important what Dudley and Goodson think.* They are genuinely *sorry* they disappointed us, but point out that they have their own lives and careers to live; and that we can come along for the ride if we can be supportive. If not, the light has turned green and they have things to do and places to go.

If you are like most other salespeople, you probably drew the *line* on how *much* distress you would *allow* yourself to *feel* in this situation, and how *much* you would allow that feeling to interfere with your life and your career. We agree. We would do the same.

Part 2

The Failure

What if we modified *two simple elements* in this story. Instead of Dudley and Goodson telling you how *we would personally prefer* to see you, we represent a well-intentioned mother, father, sister, brother, friend or spouse who influences *you* to believe it is *imperative to be seen in a new Eldorado if you are to be a person of worth and accomplishment.* Silently recite this self-belief: "I *must* be seen in an Eldorado if I am to be seen as a person of worth and accomplishment." Remember, this time you tell *yourself* it is a *requirement* to be seen in an Eldorado in order to be a person of worth and accomplishment.

It's the same mild Tuesday afternoon in your city. It has just rained and you are out driving around on business. You pull up to a red light.

There, in the next lane, you see Dudley and Goodson. There we are waiting for the light to change. We are looking straight through you with a punishing moral squint as you, in an old beat up Volkswagon bus, wait for the light to change. Looking back at us, as we obviously are looking at you, *how do you feel?* Upset? Small? Insignificant? Depressed?

The Atonement

Most salespeople say they feel upset, angry, afraid or depressed. When preference becomes *"must,"* they become *grateful* when atonement is again charitably offered. Why? Because in this situation, it makes *sense* to feel psychologically bottomed-out *if you believe* that you *must* be seen in an Eldorado, and nothing else, in order to be a person of worth. *You set yourself up by holding the belief.*

The belief implies that you are *somebody* if you have an Eldorado and are *nothing if you do not.* Emotionally, you have a perfect right to become melodramatic when you put yourself in such an all-or-nothing, live-or-die situation. Emotions prepare your body to defend against its own demise, and that is what you *allowed yourself to believe* was at stake.

Of course, the whole scenario is preposterous. Nobody would *actually* hold such beliefs, especially motivated, goal-directed salespeople. But they do. We do. You do.

What You Said You'd Never Do

The Car

How salespeople cope with the effects of such beliefs is even more peculiar. Some think it's the *car* which is at fault, not their beliefs *about* the car. So they spend a lot of time trying to get their Volkswagon bus to *pass* for a Cadillac Eldorado. The result can be bizarre.

The Intersection

Some blame the place. They cope by *continuing to drive but avoid the intersection.* In that way, they hope to escape discovery. Could that be why social differential call reluctant salespeople avoid up-market clientele?

Driving

Others give up driving *altogether.* They never venture out. They cope by killing off some of their options. In that way, they are assured that they will never have to *deal* with *any* intersection. Could that be like call reluctant salespeople who won't even *try* to prospect? They're incorrectly convinced that the *intersection* is responsible for their distress. So to avoid being distressed, they avoid the intersection.

See Me?

One group of salespeople extend the parable to even more lethal lengths. They become approval-seeking *addicts*. With chest-pounding bravado, they struggle to actually *buy* the Eldorado they *believe* they *must have* in order to have worth as a person. They anxiously wait to be seen by the Dudleys and Goodsons at intersections in cities everywhere. They *want us to see them. They need* us to see them. They dutifully wait to be wreathed in praise and repeatedly told that they are good and worthy people. But life is not necessarily fair. So Dudley and Goodson dispassionately acknowledge them and apologetically say, "So sorry. You must have missed our last memo on personal worth and accomplishment. You see, this is *Lincoln Continental week."*

Dismayed, but not disheartened, these salespeople are resolved to do what is needed to win the approval of the Dudleys and Goodsons of the world. They are true believers. They accept as *true* the misconception that they *must* have the approval of others in order to be people of worth and accomplishment. Without it, they believe they are *nothing*.

Time passes. Once again they appear at the intersection dressed in the latest Lincoln Continental. "Am I somebody yet?" their approval-seeking behavior silently queries each passerby. After a while, Dudley and Goodson show up. Anxiously we are asked, "Am I somebody of worth *now?"*

"You would have been, *five minutes ago,"* one of us answers politely, "but Lincoln Continental week just expired. Now if you want us to see you as a person of worth and accomplishment, you must purchase a new *Mercedes-Benz.* This is *foreign car week."* Still aspiring to please, they rush off without thought or reflection. They just kick up dust and go. Little do they know that we have just been reading about the exciting new work Lee Iacocca has been doing at Chrysler.

The futility of believing that feelings of self-worth can be based on *anyone else's* expectations is a popular misconception that is easier to see in others than in ourselves. It is a never-ending treadmill.

Your worth as a person is not something you win, or are ever really in danger of losing. It is *asserted* by God. It may occupy the imperfect attention of imperfect men and provide matter for their speculation, but it is *never appreciably changed in any way*.

It is *nice* to meet the expectations of others. It is even nice, for a number of objective reasons, to be able to enjoy the ownership of a Cadillac Eldorado. But that ownership does not confer acceptability, credibility or worth—it's just a nice car. If you *believe* it is an instrument that can buy the lasting approval of others, you limit it and you limit yourself. You limit the Cadillac because to you it ceases to be a car. Instead, it has become the currency of self-worth and must be vigilantly monitored, managed and *seen*. That leaves little room for enjoyment. You limit yourself by believing you must meet *other* people's expectations *before* you can allow yourself to feel worthwhile.

In actuality, your worth is a God-given *constant*. It needs to be recognized, not discovered. So why not do what you insisted you would do when we began this parable. Say, "I see the light has turned green. If you can be supportive of who I am and what I do, then come along for the ride. If you cannot, I'm sorry I disappointed you but I must be off now. I have a life to live and a career to enjoy."

One Final Word

There are always some people who aspire to judge your worth. *They're* out there, somewhere, waiting at the intersections of your life. Poised. Watching. And this could be *Batmobile week*.

RECORD YOUR PROGRESS

Most salespeople have found it very useful to maintain a daily contact initiation diary. Whenever you experience a goal-limiting feeling when you are prospecting, stop and write in your log: (1) where you *are* and what you are *doing*, (2) what you are *feeling*, (3) how you would have *coped* with that feeling in the *past*, (4) any underlying *belief(s)*, accompanying self-talk, pictures or other alarming sensations which are present, (5) things you could do or say to yourself to challenge the validity of those things, (6) what behavioral steps you *could* take, (7) the steps you actually *did* take. Set yours up like the one below.

Contact Initiation Log

Where I *am* and what I am *doing* (PAE):_____

_____

_____

What I am *feeling* (PFC): _____

_____

_____

How I *used to* cope: _____

_____

_____

Active beliefs, pictures, self-talk (STT): _____

_____

_____

Things I can say to *challenge* validity: _____

_____

_____

Things I *could* do: _____

_____

_____

What I actually *did do*: _____

_____

_____

Keep your Contact Initiation Log for at least three weeks. It does take time, and it does mean more paper work, *but it also really helps.* So carry it with you and review it at the end of each work day.

ONE FINAL CHECK

Let's see if we can identify some of the self-limiting self-talk behind some of the actual statements we have heard during our years of teaching at the Call Reluctance Center. Read each statement carefully. Then decide whether you think the statement is goal-supporting or goal-obstructing. Be careful. Some are tricky. Try to read between the lines. Look for underlying sources of self-pressurization.

Example

1. "To be a success in this business you *have got to* have a positive mental attitude." Goal-Enhancing? Goal-Obstructing?

     Answer: Goal-Obstructing. It would be *nice* to have a positive outlook. Reasonable people prefer one over a negative, gloomy outlook. But the statement above is *goal-obstructing* for two reasons. First, it is *simply not true*. There are many top producers in every industry who are *anything but* positive. Some are morose! Just talking to them is like entering a mausoleum. Their success and outlook on life are clearly unrelated. Their outlook does *not necessarily help nor hinder* their performance. Even so, we would still rather be positive than negative. But it's *our choice*, not a requirement.

     Secondly, in the statement above, attitude has become elevated *over production*. Some salespeople believe they *cannot* prospect or work *unless* and *until* they have a positive mental attitude. In that sense, the statement takes a desirable attitude and makes it career-obstructive.

     Now it's your turn. See what you can find in the following self-statements. Decide for yourself if they contain the seeds of self-growth or self-defeat. The answers are at the end of the exercise. Additionally, if you have the time, alone or with a group of your colleagues, determine what you would say to each of these people if you were their sales manager. How would you help them discover what they are really saying to themselves? How would you help them to see the effect the statement has on their ability to prospect? ACTION BREAK.

2. "The last call I made got me so mad I can't call anybody else. But I'll get even. I'll call that miserable scum every hour on the hour till dawn!"

3. "I can't make calls until I get organized!"

4. "I'd like to learn as much as I can as fast as I can, but I've only been in this business for six months now and reasonable people won't expect me to know everything."

5. "How can you expect me to prospect right now? I'm not in the mood. You lied to me about this career, about the hours I'd have to keep, and about how much money I'd make. God will get you for that!"

6. "When I make the Top Performers Club I'll have it made. I'll be up there with the big boys. Then I'll feel more confident because people won't be doubting my ability."

7. "Sure, I would like to have the respect of all the people I try to call on. But I know that I don't have to have it to do a good job."

8. "I've finally landed. I just know that this guy will manage me right. Now I can prospect because I have finally found a career that is going to make me happy!"

9. "I feel so terrible I can't work. Bob, one of my good friends who I influenced to come into this business, is doing very badly and I'm really upset."

10. "I can't really cut myself loose and begin to prospect until I know that this is really the right career for me."

Answers:

> Goal-Supporting: 4,7
> Goal-Obstructing: 2,3,5,6,8,9,10

WHAT NEXT?

Now, turn to the next Rx section(s) prescribed for *your particular type of call reluctance.*

*The principle behind
this process is simple but
elegant. As you lower
your fear response to that
which you fear least
about prospecting, your
greater fears about pros-
pecting will automatically
be lowered by the same
degree.*

R_x TWO

THREAT DESENSITIZATION

PRIMARILY AFFECTS:	PRESCRIBED FOR:
Thoughts	**X Threat Sensitivity**
	Desurgency
Feelings	Protension
	X Groups
X Actions	Personal Friends
	Disruption Sensitivity
	Social Differential
	Role Acceptance
	Family/Relatives

A BRIEF OVERVIEW

Threat Desensitization consists of a group of procedures for coping with people and situations which threaten your daily prospecting performance and, for one reason or another, are resistant to change.

How Does Threat Desensitization Work?

Threat Desensitization is a simple, four-step process. By seriously directing your motivation towards the disciplined application of these steps, you will minimize the emotional effort it takes to initiate sales calls. The four steps are:

1. Learning to relax *on cue*

2. Composing a *list* of those things associated with prospecting which presently trigger your automatic fear response

3. Composing a list of feared prospecting situations and *ranking* them from most fearful to least fearful

4. Learning to move through your ranked list without experiencing immobilizing fear

Guiding Principles
Behind Threat Desensitization

1. *You are motivated* to learn more effective means of coping with threat-sensitive call reluctance.

2. *Your motivation is goal-directed* and you desire to overcome threat-sensitive call reluctance in order to improve your prospecting activity.

3. Threat-sensitive call reluctance is the product of inborn fight/flight mechanisms combined with learned reactions to perceived threats.

4. Your call reluctant *response(s)* to specific things, people and situations was learned and, therefore, can be unlearned.

5. Two contradictory feelings cannot be present at the same time; therefore, an individual cannot be simultaneously threatened and relaxed.

6. You can learn to tolerate, cope with and even become accustomed to most prospecting circumstances regardless of the degree of the perceived threat.

Sighting the Target

This procedure works best with *specific, chronic fears and phobias* such as distress associated with the use of the telephone for prospecting. It is not recommended for use with generalized fears such as a "sense of dread," "low self-confidence," or "fear of failure."

Estimated Completion Time

The preparatory relaxation sequence and development of a Perceived Prospecting Threat Inventory: 5-6 days

Ability to visualize threatening prospecting situations without triggering a fear reaction: 1-2 weeks

Ability to approach actual prospecting situations without triggering a fear response: 2-3 weeks

HOW TO APPLY THREAT DESENSITIZATION

Step One: Learning to Relax

Learning to relax is the cornerstone upon which threat desensitization rests. Some salespeople are at first inclined to ridicule procedures like the one you are about to learn. If you are one of these, we ask your patience and momentary cooperation, for this skill is a vital first step for neutralizing your automatic fear reactions to specific prospecting situations.

You are about to learn how to relax body muscle groups by tensing and releasing them while you recite a relaxation cue. This cue will then become paired with the *sensation* of relaxation that you experience when you release muscle tension.

To begin, find a quiet, nondistracting place and make yourself comfortable. You can either lie down or sit in a comfortable chair. You may wish to read the following relaxation dialogue into a tape recorder which you can play back whenever you want to practice the exercise.

If you have recorded the instructions, turn the recorder on and close your eyes.

Relaxation Dialogue

Begin by clenching your right fist tightly. Notice how you can allow yourself to feel the other parts of your body as you feel the pressure in your right hand. Visualize your right hand clenched into a fist. Now let yourself become momentarily aware of how you are breathing and how you can feel the tension growing in your hand and up your forearm as you see your clenched fist grow tighter. Now imagine that you are looking at your fist through a large pair of binoculars. The binoculars have a special button on top of the lens near the front. Don't press it yet, but when you do, it will flash a large, multi-colored sign in front of your eyes that says "SET." The message "SET" is designed to automatically stay on for only two seconds. Then it will automatically turn itself off until you press it again. If you will not allow yourself to see the word "SET," then just pretend you see it.

As you feel your tightened right fist, take a deep breath and hold it for five seconds . . . now allow yourself to slowly exhale. At the moment you begin to exhale, depress the imaginary button one time. As you see yourself pressing the button, you can see the word "SET," and as you do, slowly begin to relax your right hand. When it is relaxed, touch your left index finger to your thumb and say to yourself, "RELAX." Pause for about a minute. Now clench your right hand again, take another deep breath and hold it for five seconds . . . exhale, then press the imaginary button so you again see the word "SET" as you are exhaling and slowly releasing the pressure from your right hand.

When your hand is relaxed, again touch your left index finger to your left thumb and say "RELAX." Pause for another minute, then continue the sequence one more time: Clench, deep breath, hold for five, press the button, see the word "SET," exhale and continue to slowly release the pressure from your hand until it is totally limp. Then, again touch your left index finger to your left thumb and say the word "RELAX." Now, just pause. Don't do anything for five minutes except to breathe deeply. Don't even try to notice how different your hand now feels compared to how it felt when it was clenched.

The ability to solicit your automatic relaxation response at will is the key to many stress reduction programs. It also plays an important part in other procedures in this book. Hence, it is important that you do not skim through the procedure. If you have threat-sensitive call reluctance, and want to correct it, the battle starts right here, right now.

An Effective Short Cut To Relaxation

Most practitioners of relaxation techniques begin by relaxing a toe or a hand. They then move through every part of the body step-by-step. The method taught here, however, is a short cut. We have learned from years of experience that for our limited purposes we can achieve the same results with much less effort and in much less time. How? By teaching you a *code word* (SET) which prepares you to relax by first focusing your attention on relaxation. The word is not the process of relaxation itself. It merely *signals* you to focus your attention upon the process so that your relaxation response can then be easily triggered by the *cue word* (RELAX). Since you cannot relax and be tense at the same time, it logically follows that the relaxation response should spread throughout the body. With practice, your relaxation response can be called upon at will. When you find yourself in a potentially threatening situation, you can call up your relaxation response by saying your code word (SET) followed by your cue word (RELAX), and your body will reexperience the entire relaxation sequence.

Step Two: Developing
Your Prospecting Threat Inventory

When we say that prospecting threatens us, what we really mean is that certain *aspects* of prospecting set off automatic fear responses which vary from person to person. What aspects of prospecting set off *your* automatic fear responses? What aspects of prospecting do *you* see as threatening? Take a few minutes to compile a list of all the people, situations and things associated with prospecting that you avoid or fear because you perceive them as potential threats.

Here is a partial list completed by Tom L, an experienced stockbroker, during a session at the Call Reluctance Center:

Prospecting Threat Inventory

1. *Preparing* to make a cold call

2. *Making* a cold call

3. Just *thinking* about making a cold call

4. *Showing up late* for the first sales appointment

5. *Being unprepared* for questions I might be asked

6. *Being watched* by my sales trainer as I give a prospecting presentation

7. *Not knowing* who will answer the phone

8. *Contacting someone who just had a bad experience* with the last salesman that contacted him

9. *Getting sick* while I'm there

10. *Calling someone who is already mad* for some other reason

11. Trying to psych myself up for the call, then *having a bad experience on the phone* and getting depressed

12. *Being ridiculed* or made a fool of

13. *Dropping my sales script* in the middle of a phone presentation

14. *Being forced to make a call* by my trainer before I say I'm ready

As you can see, Tom's list (which was actually much longer) contains several *themes*. The most obvious is cold-calling on the telephone. Now take a few minutes and construct your own Prospecting Threat Inventory. It can be as long or as short as you like. But be sure to list all the threatening things which come to mind about prospecting. Then look for the themes that are present in your inventory. If you cannot think of *anything*, then just *pretend, but go through the exercise.* ACTION BREAK.

The Self-Interview Approach

What themes emerge from your list? Cold calling? Using the phone? Asking for referrals? Being found unprepared? Sometimes it is hard to take a candid and objective look at ourselves. But the success of this procedure rests in part upon your having done that. So let's take a moment to play a mind game. Pretend you are a highly paid training consultant hired to review a very special case, *yours*. Interview yourself from the consultant's objective perspective. In front of a mirror, ask yourself what prospecting situations frighten you the most. Check if anything should have been included on the list that was omitted. If so, go ahead and add it to your list. Threat-sensitive salespeople sometimes find that completing a *thorough* list can take several days. So give yourself all the time you need. But be careful! *Do not let the part of you which is call reluctant sabotage your efforts by insisting on a perfect list. That's a decoy tactic to keep you from completing your inventory. Don't fall for it!*

Step Three: Threat Ranking

Select any one of the themes from your inventory. On a separate piece of paper, copy everything from your list that relates to that theme. Then ask yourself, "Which one do I fear the most?" and assign it 100 prospecting distress points. It's important that you really get into the situation and make it as real as your imagination will allow. Try to observe as much detail as you can about the people, places, events and sensations associated with the situation. Then do the same thing with the *least* threatening item on your list and assign it ten prospecting distress points. Now all you need to do is fill in the middle ground between least and most threatening. The following is an example of an actual list. Look it over and then complete your own. ACTION BREAK.

Tom L, Stockbroker
Theme from Prospecting Threat Inventory:
Using the phone to prospect

Threatening Situations	Prospecting Distress Points
Getting into an argument with a prospect on the phone	50
Picking up the phone	85
Dialing the phone	60
Hearing the phone ring on the other end	40
Hearing the individual on the other end say "Hello"	100
Having a secretary answer the phone	70
Having the secretary ask me what the call "is in regards to"	75
Looking at the clock and realizing in 5 minutes I'm supposed to be on the phone prospecting	30
Hearing Bob and John talk about how many calls they just finished making	20
Seeing the number of phone calls my trainer listed for my daily objective.	15

Notice that the *most* threatening item on Tom's list (100 distress points) is dialing the phone and hearing someone on the other end say "Hello." The *least* threatening item (15 distress points) is seeing the number of calls his trainer assigned for the day.

Step Four: Moving through the Ranks

So far we have done the following: 1) Learned to relax on cue, 2) taken an inventory of those things that threaten us about prospecting, 3) identified distressful theme areas in our inventory, and 4) selected one theme and assigned prospecting distress points to each individual part.

What you have done so far has been in preparation for what comes next. You are about to *imagine* that you are in your least threatening situation. With the help of the following procedure, try to hold this image until you no longer experience the immobilizing distress that you normally feel in that situation.

The principle behind this process is simple but elegant. As you lower your fear response to the least threatening element on your list, the *other elements will automatically be lowered by the same degree.* Some people get used to the water at the beach this way. They slowly immerse themselves a little at a time until they are completely wet. Though the water may seem cold at first, once completely wet, they find it hard to imagine that the water ever was cold enough to be uncomfortable. Threat Desensitization works the same way *if you closely follow the steps below.*

1. Find a place where you can be alone and will not be distracted for several minutes. Have the threat ranking exercise you just completed handy.

2. Assume a comfortable position. Use your code word (SET) and your cue word (RELAX) to allow yourself to become more relaxed.

3. Preferably with your eyes closed, allow your mind to visualize the *least* threatening item on your threat ranking list. Once you can see it, pretend to make it as *real as possible.* Notice any sensations you would experience if you were actually in that situation. Pretend to hear what you would actually hear if you were in that situation. Pretend to see the things you would see and smell the things you would smell.

4. Be alert for any sign of distress regardless of how subtle it may be. Once you feel any distress, take a deep breath. Then use your code word to focus your attention and your cue word to relax.

5. Notice any difference in how you allow yourself to feel. If you like the difference, anchor it by saying to yourself, "I can see myself in this situation, but now I will allow myself to be more relaxed."

6. Pause. Turn the scene off for a moment. Try to think only of the color gray, or just allow your mind to drift, but do not become too relaxed.

7. Repeat steps one through six again. Can you visualize the same scene again? Is it any clearer? What changes in the scene do you allow yourself to notice?

8. Once you have been able to go through steps one through six *three times in a row* while experiencing as little distress as you will allow, you can then proceed to repeat the process with the next higher item on your Prospecting Threat Inventory theme.

Walking Through the Process with Tom L

Let's see how Tom, our stockbroker, did with the above process. Tom had difficulty allowing other people to know how he was actually feeling. He even had trouble admitting that he needed help with his prospecting. Thus, since this procedure is self-administered, it was especially suitable for Tom.

He followed instructions by first removing himself from the ebb and flow of human enterprise. He practiced at home just before bedtime or in an empty office during his lunch hour. At first it was difficult for him to visualize a threatening scene from his inventory. So, thinking that he had found a loophole in the exercise, he compliantly *pretended* to visualize the situation as instructed. This is how he related his experience to a group of salespeople at the Call Reluctance Center:

> "After a few minutes, something funny happened. I forgot I was pretending and the whole scene began to play just like I was really there. When I realized I wasn't pretending anymore, it kind of hit me like one of those insights we get about ourselves from time to time. And along with that insight came another one. I realized that I could visualize anything I wanted to, including the things that scare me about prospecting. I just didn't want to see them, and I didn't like the idea of other people telling me to picture something I don't want to see."

Tom proceeded to use his code and cue.

> "Earlier they had taught me how to do the code and cue thing, but for the life of me I couldn't see what good it was going to do for me."

He was soon to find out.

> "As the scene got real to me, I did begin to feel some of the things I feel when I'm really sitting there listening to Steve, my trainer, tell me how many calls I'm supposed to make before the day is over. I could feel myself begin to fidget and tighten up all over. It became so real for me that I began to see and hear myself do what I always do, begin to make an excuse or change the subject or something. But then I remembered I was supposed to use my code and cue thing they taught me. I took a few quick deep breaths and then said SET and RELAX. It was fabulous. Almost immediately I could feel myself loosening up all over my body, just like my fist felt when I stopped clenching it. It was great. Once I could see what was happening, I practiced until I could get all the way through seeing my trainer giving me phone calling objectives for the day without

feeling any reaction. It took me four times to get through it, but once I got up to speed I moved through the rest of the list fast. Hearing the prospect answer the phone used to scare the hell out of me. I can honestly say that I got to where they (prospects) could say anything they wanted to and it wouldn't bother me."

You may be more or less successful than Tom. If the process comes easy, try moving through three or four items on your list in one sitting. Remember, however, to go through each item as many times as necessary until you can visualize the scene with as little distress as possible. Be sure to stop for the day if you feel bored, annoyed or overly distressed.

APPLICATION IN REAL LIFE PROSPECTING

So far, the procedure has only been applied in your head. But what happens when you face these prospecting threats in the real world? To your mind, there is very little difference between what you have rehearsed during this process and an actual prospecting situation; your mind does not qualitatively distinguish between the two. Your reaction to many of the events which once were threatening will now be markedly reduced or eliminated. This is because you have reengineered your mind to handle these situations, *real or imagined.*

Tom never learned to enjoy using the phone to prospect, but he did learn to stop fearing it. Today he uses it, along with other prospecting tools, to further his already successful career as a stockbroker.

"I didn't think much of it (the procedure) on paper. But lucky for me I gave it a try. I won't say that it will work for everybody. But it worked for me, and if it could work for somebody like me, it ought to be able to work for damn near everybody."

DEBRIEFING AND PROGRESS MAINTENANCE

Debriefing has two purposes. The first is to help you determine what worked best for you so you can apply the procedure more effectively in the future if you should need a booster shot. The second is to find out what went wrong if you did not benefit from the procedure as much as you would like.

Your debriefing may be more effective if you have a friend interview you about your struggle with threat sensitive call reluctance and your recent experience with Threat Desensitization. If that is not possible, then interview yourself. Ask yourself the following questions and record your answers into a tape recorder for later review.

Debriefing Questions

- Did you apply this procedure alone, in a group, with a professional counselor, or with the help of a friend?

- Tell me about the use of the code and cue words. What are they and how do they work?

- What are the prospecting-related situations, people and things that formerly distressed you?

- Can you describe what it was like when distressful feelings blocked your career?

- What was the purpose of threat ranking?

- How did you go about threat ranking?

- How many times did you use your code and cue words with your least threatening item before you would allow yourself to feel less distressed?

- Did learning to *visualize* yourself prospecting with less distress result in less distress in the real life prospecting situation?

- Overall, do you think your experience with Threat Desensitization was a positive one?

- How closely did you follow the instructions?

- Do you have any other thoughts or feelings about your experience with Threat Desensitization?

Repeat the debriefing section if you think you need a booster shot. If you catch yourself regressing to the old response habits, repeat the entire procedure. Over the years, we have found that some threat-sensitive salespeople need to use this procedure about once a year. For others, like the authors who are not naturally outgoing personalities and who are naturally predisposed to acquiring threat sensitive call reluctance, an inoculation of this procedure is required quarterly. For most threat sensitive salespeople, however, one shot will probably last your entire career.

*J*ulia was addicted to the pleasures of escaping from any prospecting situation she feared. She was an avoidance junkie. Whereas some people get hooked on alcohol or sugar, others get hooked on the momentary pleasures associated with a successful escape.

R̲x̲ THREE

NEGATIVE IMAGE PROJECTION

PRIMARILY AFFECTS:

X Thoughts

X Feelings

Actions

PRESCRIBED FOR:

Threat Sensitivity
Desurgency
Protension
Groups
X Personal Friends
Disruption Sensitivity
X Social Differential
Role Acceptance
X Family/Relatives

A BRIEF OVERVIEW

One of the chief characteristics of any self-crippling habit is the short-term *relief, gain* or *pleasure* it produces. This is why negative habits persist. Certain forms of call reluctance work the same way. For example, Personal Friends, Family/Relatives and Social Differential types of call reluctance feature habitual evasions which provide momentary escape and relief.

The Case of Julia Z, Avoidance Junkie

Julia Z was a salesperson with social differential call reluctance. She tried to initiate contact with presidents and owners of medium and large organizations to sell her company's line of mini-computers. But Julia feared the very prospects she had to call on. She experienced short-term *relief* when her cluttered social life interfered with her scheduled prospecting activities. Curiously, distracting social activities managed to surface almost every afternoon. Julia thought she was disorganized, scatterbrained or possibly suffering from signs of early senility. But a closer look at her avoidance behavior revealed a very organized and highly disciplined commitment. Her manager, in an attempt to help, sent her to two different time management and goal setting courses. They failed, though not entirely because of *their* shortcomings.

Julia was psychologically *addicted* to the pleasures of escaping from any prospecting situation she feared. She was an *avoidance junkie.* Some people get hooked on alcohol, some on sugar, others on the momentary pleasures associated with a successful escape. Paradoxically, salespeople like Julia get a momentary sense of relief when they successfully avoid having to prospect. But the escape exacts a heavy toll. In the case of Julia, it resulted in her prospecting becoming even more difficult and emotionally charged; she fell behind in her prospecting activity and ran out of people to sell to. Julia's sales career fell apart. And worst of all, her failure could have been avoided had she been aware of Negative Image Projection.

How Does Negative Image Projection Work?

Negative Image Projection is a mental process you can apply to yourself. It is based on the understanding that self-limiting habits become strengthened *by repetition and association with sensations of immediate relief.* Therefore, the key to eliminating these habits is to disconnect them from the momentary gain that accompanies them. This is done by *repeatedly* associating the habit with obnoxious (negative) mental imagery. After some repetition, the old habit will no longer be bonded to its pleasant sensations. Instead, it will be habitually linked to disgusting, noxious and repulsive images. Under these circumstances, *prospecting becomes the more desirable choice.*

Guiding Principles
Behind Negative Image Projection

1. *You are motivated* to overcome call reluctant reactions to prospecting.

2. To improve your prospecting activity, *your motivation is directed* specifically towards reducing unwanted distressful feelings associated with self-promotion.

3. Feelings can enhance or impede the flow of motivation towards goal-directed behaviors.

4. Habits of escape result in momentary feelings of relief.

5. Relief from having to prospect feels good and reinforces the method you use to evade prospecting.

6. Pairing your evasive behavior with a *pleasant* sensation (relief) *increases* the likelihood that you will use that behavior *again.*

7. Repeated evasions become *habits* which, like all habits, grow stronger when repeated and reinforced.

8. Habits can be eliminated if the link between them and the pleasant sensations they evoke is *broken.*

Sighting the Target

Negative Image Projection is particularly suited to call reluctant habits which interfere with prospecting highly targeted groups such as family, friends and up-market clientele. It is not recommended for more generalized forms of call reluctance such as Threat Sensitivity or Desurgency. It is easy to learn and many salespeople have even enjoyed using it.

Estimated Completion Time

Meaningful results will take about a week, though some salespeople have reported lasting results within a few days.

POSITIVE ATTITUDE VS. NEGATIVE IMAGES

If you survey the many available self-help books, cassettes and articles on this subject, you will find that most of them emphasize self-confidence and positive mental attitude as the essential foundations for a successful career in sales. The only exception we know of is *How To Cure Yourself of Positive Thinking* by Donald G. Smith. Thus, we are somewhat reluctant to introduce a skill for using *negative* images to correct certain forms of call reluctance which are popularly believed to come from negative attitudes in the first place. Nevertheless, try to suspend judgement and we will explain why we think you will find this to be the preferred procedure for correcting the three types of call reluctance mentioned previously.

LUNCH WITH KEVIN AND BRIAN

Brian T, a young consultant for a prominent sales training firm, is still enjoying a lunch which started at 11:30. It's now 1:15. Brian realizes that one of his responsibilities as a trainer-consultant is to generate new business. This requires him to spend time in the office on the telephone, *something he should be doing now.* But he and Kevin, one of his co-workers, feel obligated to order another vodka and tonic to soften the afternoon's phone calls. As usual, Brian knows better but offers no resistance as he lifts his glass towards their waitress and says, "Fill it up with premium."

Both Brian and Kevin are motivated, goal-directed salespeople. Neither, however, are producing new business at a satisfactory level. Harold "Bubba" Kline, their manager, is getting weary of repeatedly pointing out to them that they spend too much time at lunch and on breaks and not enough time calling on prospective clients. And their production shows it.

Neither are alcoholics, so why don't they stop? The next round of drinks will waste valuable prospecting time. Plus, when they *do* return to the office, their productivity will be low. And by three or four in the afternoon, they will experience episodes of energy-sapping stress as they struggle to catch up.

Let's put this situation under a microscope. As Brian and Kevin sit and discuss the afternoon's prospecting, multiple images pass in mental review, images of calling on up-market clientele. Accompanying the images are *negative* memories and sensations. So when another drink is suggested as an alternative to prospecting, both Brian and Kevin flash to a new set of mental images paired to a glass of crystal clear liquid anesthetic. These images are potent and beguilingly pleasant. This ritual occurs whenever Brian and Kevin have lunch together prior to an afternoon of prospecting. And since they lunch together every day, this scene is replayed, and the escape route is strengthened, *day after day after day after day. . .*

A FEW OTHER PLEASANT ESCAPES

The same thing happens when you shuffle prospect cards instead of contacting personal friends who you know would be interested in your product. But wouldn't they feel that you were taking advantage of their friendship? If you have family/ friends call reluctance, your answer is "yes," but it doesn't stop there. You actually project the images and feel the sensations that you *think* your friends will experience if they feel exploited by you. By contrast, the prospect cards feel better than making the call, so you momentarily escape by shuffling and reshuffling the cards.

The same thing happens when you refuse to contact a relative who needs your company's services. Instead of making the call, you feel compelled to escape from images of yourself not being taken seriously and sensations of embarrassment and shame. To cope, you search for a more pleasant image. You see yourself shooting the bull with your friends in the canteen and feel the comforting warmth of coffee in your mouth, sliding down your throat, and warming the bottom of your stomach. Prospecting cannot successfully compete with such escapist imagery. Bali Hai is calling. . .

BREAKING THE BOND

Busting pleasurable habits associated with escaping from things we wish to *avoid* is different than eliminating habits like smoking, nail biting or nervous tics. Why? Because these pleasurable habits provide immediate *gain* in the form of momentary escape (relief) from the emotional distress of prospecting. So how do you break a habit which produces a feeling you *like* as opposed to dislike? By transforming the outcome from a positive to a negative sensation, from relief to repulsion, from psychic pleasure to psychic pain.

Step One: Relax On Command

The first step in using Negative Image Projection is to learn how to allow yourself to relax on command. You can do this by referring to "Step One: Learning To Relax" in the chapter on Threat Desensitization.

Step Two: Examine Your Escape Route

Next, closely examine the escape habit you use to avoid prospecting. *Think about* your escape route. Do you pretend to be sick? Do you lie to your manager? Do you shuffle prospect cards? Do you stay longer on coffee breaks than you should? Do you go on endless searches for *more* information? Localize the event. Where are you located when you feel the need to escape? What are you doing? Who are you with, if anyone? For Brian, when lunch approaches, can prospecting be far away? His thoughts seek out a more tolerable theme.

Step Three: Fill In The Details

Now relax. Fill in the details of your prospecting escape route. List in sequence all the pleasurable things associated with your escape route. Be detailed. Be graphic. Be explicit.

Fifteen minutes prior to lunch, Brian begins to see *images* of himself entering the restaurant, reviewing the menu, placing the order with the waitress, holding the glass of vodka and tonic, and having an enjoyable conversation with Kevin. He mentally rehearses his escape before he actually arrives at lunch.

As you imagine going through your escape route, it would be helpful to number each step along the way for later use.

Step Four: List Your Repulsers

The next step is to compile a list of things which immediately repulse you whenever you think of them. Everybody has some. To make the job easier, we have listed some suggestions below. Take out a piece of paper and copy those items from our list which are especially repulsive to you. Feel free to add any of your own.

The Repulser Sampler

- Fingernails screeching across a blackboard
- Painful injection by needle directly into your stomach
- Kissing the face of a dead person whose eyes are open and looking directly at you
- Your dentist deep-drilling your teeth
- Open, infected, running wounds
- Standing several stories up and looking straight down with nothing to hang onto
- Stench of dead, decaying animals on a hot day
- Having blood drawn directly from an artery in your neck
- Sinking neck-deep into a pit of slimy, slithering snakes
- Insects crawling into your mouth while you are sound asleep
- Vomiting uncontrollably in a restaurant
- Unknowingly stepping on a live rat
- Absentmindedly saying a sexual obscenity while making a presentation to an auditorium full of family members
- Knowing a spider has dropped down your shirt (or blouse) during an important presentation and not being able to scream or get it out
- Unknowingly squashing live worms underfoot as you walk into a dark room

Select as many items from the list of repulsers as there are steps in your escape route. Choose only those items which turn you off the most. (If any of the above items turn you on, there are other books you should be reading.) The items you choose should produce distinct sensory impressions which result in clear physical sensations. Don't play safe. These choices are important. The procedure will only work if your selections cause you to be grossed out.

Step Six: Applying Your Repulsers

This step depends upon your success with the previous two steps (breaking down the pleasurable components in your escape route and selecting your repulsers). Connect each step of your escape route to one of your repulsers, creating narrative pairs similar to this: "I shuffle my prospect cards, and the more I fondle them, the more . . . *I can smell the stench of dead, decaying animals on a hot summer's day.*"

Here is how Brian broke the habit of social drinking in lieu of telephone prospecting. He started by mentally rehearsing the escape scene. He remembered and imagined each good sensation he felt while escaping. Then, when he had the first item of his escape route in mind, and felt the pleasant sensations which accompanied it, he inserted one of the repulsers which immediately and dramatically changed his reaction from pleasure to disgust.

"I saw myself getting ready to order the next drink. Fondling the menu. Glancing at the waitress's legs. Looking into her face. Hearing Kevin ask me to order one more. Placing the order. *Then I saw this guy who always sat in a nearby booth. He was unremarkable in every respect but one: He had the ugliest, open running wounds I have ever seen covering both arms. He was a real gross-out. I wanted to leave right then and there.*"

"Next, I saw myself enjoying the drink. Feeling the glass. Tasting it. Feeling the warmth as it slid down my throat. Listening to Kevin complain about his boss and his job in general. *Then I saw myself being drawn down neck-deep into a pit of slippery, wet snakes. I wanted to get out of there real bad. Then I smelled the stench of dead and decaying animals which were under the table. The smell was gagging. I thought I was going to vomit all over the restaurant table. I told Kevin that I had to leave and immediately got the hell out of there. Heading back to the office, the air felt refreshing and I felt good and relaxed once again.*"

Make sure that you stop the repulser as soon as you stop the pleasurable habit. Then allow yourself to feel relief and relaxation.

Now you are ready to apply the relaxation skill you learned in step one. After you have paired repulsers with pleasure points in your escape route, relax and close your eyes. Dwell on the first escape item. Fix it clearly in your mind. Pretend to be there. Hear the sounds. Smell the odors. Feel the textures. Taste the flavors. Then, when you have the scene in mind, go *immediately* to the paired repulser. Once you have the repulser in mind, stay with it for at least a few seconds or until you have displaced any pleasurable sensations associated with the first escape item. Progress through each item on your escape route until you have successfully experienced pairing all of them with a repulser.

Step Seven: Disengaging the Repulsers

Relive your escape scenario again. But this time avoid the repulsers by imagining yourself sidestepping the once pleasurable escape route and making your calls instead.

As soon as you feel the need to fondle your prospect cards, as opposed to using them one at a time to make calls, you will begin to smell the stench of death and decay. But you can make it go away by going directly to the telephone and making calls. Repeat the sequence several times, pairing the prospect cards with immediate use of the telephone. You will soon learn that it is easier to make calls than to remain totally grossed out.

A REVIEW AND FINAL STEP

Let's review the essential steps:

1. Build a detailed description of your escape route.

2. Just as you begin to enjoy the pleasure of escaping, introduce a repulser.

3. Continue to pair repulsers to the escape route until you permit yourself to sidestep the escape route in favor of making calls. At that time, and only at that time, stop using the repulsers.

You have learned how to make the pleasure of escape disgusting. But by doing so, you have not made prospecting any more enjoyable. To do that, whenever you successfully make a call as opposed to avoiding it, list three things you are moved closer to realizing or obtaining because you made the call. Do that immediately after you make each call regardless of its outcome.

Watch out for _under-standing_. The compulsion to understand everything about call reluctance can get you into serious trouble. Dance around it. It's a booby trap.

R͟x͟ FOUR

FEAR INVERSION

PRIMARILY AFFECTS:	PRESCRIBED FOR:
Thoughts	Threat Sensitivity
	X Desurgency
Feelings	**X Protension**
	Groups
X Actions	Personal Friends
	Disruption Sensitivity
	Social Differential
	Role Acceptance
	Family/Relatives

A BRIEF OVERVIEW

Motivation empowers us. As it flows through us, it provides the potential for accomplishing our goals. But sometimes our motivation gets misdirected or interrupted. Wires get crossed. Sparks arc across conflicting intentions and our energy is pirated away to other purposes. The result is a motivational short circuit. With behaviors as complex as protensive call reluctance, the flow of motivational energy gets reversed. Instead of energizing us to greater levels of achievement, it turns angrily back on itself. Our options become limited to a few rigid counter-productive parodies of our true talent and ability.

Of all the known procedures for dealing with protensive call reluctance, Fear Inversion is the one found to be the most helpful. But unlike the other procedures in this book, Fear Inversion is a blind application. It must be applied without an explanation of what it is or how it works.

Guiding Principles Behind Fear Inversion

1. You admit that protensive call reluctance is a problem which limits your prospecting.

2. You are motivated to improve.

3. You, like all salespeople, have choices.

4. Much of what you are today and will be tomorrow is due to choices you make.

5. Although you are influenced by instinct, inheritance, predisposition and your sales environment, you can still exercise the freedom to choose within those preconditions.

6. Some salespeople are afraid to be afraid.

7. If you fearfully anticipate an event, you insure that when the event actually occurs it will frighten you.

8. You already have the knowledge, motivation and discipline you need in order to change. It has just been misdirected.

9. In dealing with protensive call reluctance, the pursuit of understanding and self-knowledge is wasteful and usually futile.

10. Taking responsibility for what you do, rather than what you know, is the essential building block.

11. You have at least a minimal imagination.

12. You have at least a minimal ability to tolerate ambiguity and follow instructions.

Sighting the Target

Fear Inversion is based on your inclination to act in opposites. It will not change your life, only your prospecting behavior. It is fast and very powerful. It is particularly suited for salespeople with protensive call reluctance who may be coping with problems like anxiety attacks, fear of "going crazy," extreme social embarrassment, fear of being exposed for who they "really" are, or loss of self-control. It works quickly and sometimes very dramatically because it does not rely on *understanding*. It targets the way that you ineffectively cope. In addition to Protension, it may also be effective with desurgent call reluctance. It is not particularly suited for any other types.

Estimated Completion Time

Used correctly, Fear Inversion is one of the fastest and most mysterious procedures in the entire arsenal of behavior change techniques. The key is to use it *correctly*. The instructions must be followed in the order given.

Side Effects

This procedure, unlike others in this book, may have side effects on some readers. Some salespeople will strongly react to the procedure by insisting that it is comically shallow, boring, beneath them, theoretically confused and that it won't work for them. If that happens to you, don't be dismayed. It's a predictable side effect. It's proof that the medicine is having an effect on your call reluctance.

Failure Rate

Success does not come easy to salespeople with protensive call reluctance, even when Fear Inversion is used. The reason is straightforward. Protensive call reluctance is much more complex than the other forms of call reluctance and requires a more complex corrective procedure. Historically, procedures like Fear Inversion are best left to professionals with specialized training in the fear of self-promotion. But go ahead and try it. You could be among the important group of exceptions. And even if you are not, you may still derive some benefit from the experience.

THE PROCESS BEGINS

Protensive call reluctance actually consists of two basic processes, *anticipation* and *covering*. Together, they combine to form one of the most vicious forms of call reluctance identified so far. Highly motivated, intelligent and creative salespeople who are coping with an *unrealistically low impression of themselves* are the most vulnerable to protensive call reluctance. It is among the most stubborn forms of call reluctance to overcome because its victims often become unwitting co-conspirators by using highly motivated, intelligent and creative *means of coping*.

Anticipation

Salespeople with protensive call reluctance fearfully anticipate certain people, prospecting events or circumstances. They set themselves up for a complete *emotional* wipe-out. If and when the event actually does occur, they are *overwhelmed by the fear they anticipated*. This distressing encounter is then used as additional *reason* to fearfully anticipate the event happening *again*. So protensive call reluctance is a *fear cycle*. The anticipation phase can become so self-restricting that some salespeople do not even want to *know* what is frightening them because they fear they would be emotionally overwhelmed if they ever found out. The plot thickens.

Covering

Salespeople with protensive call reluctance are almost always highly motivated perfectionists who are mercilessly self-critical. They tolerate some imperfection in others but refuse to allow themselves to be less than perfect in every respect. They are concerned about even *appearing* less than perfect, an awkward objective for someone who is call reluctant. And since they are afraid of being seen as weak, immature or out of control, they go to considerable lengths to hide blemishes such as call reluctance. Afraid of being afraid, they seek relative safety behind a facade of superior taste, intellectual ability, and the appearance of internal strength. Over the years, they may grow to gradually believe and passionately defend their cover while feeling fragmented and unsure of how and when it all began. The weaker a protensive salesperson *believes* he or she is, the more he or she is likely to feel the need for a *cover*. Thus, the amount of motivation diverted to covering a perceived deficiency is proportionate to the *perceived* need to compensate for being just the opposite. For example, a protensive salesperson *who thinks* that prospects might hold his advice in low esteem may *cover* by growing a Freudian beard and liberally sprinkling his conversation with psychobabble. Another who believes her competence might be suspect, may *cover* by papering her office with ego inflating decals like degrees, awards, plaques and certificates. Yet another who *thinks* his worth is suspect, may costume himself in designer clothes, join a country club, and endlessly drop the names of influential people he knows or just knows of. Sound familiar?

Prospecting Charades

If you have protensive call reluctance, you are probably investing too much energy in your image and not enough in fundamentals like prospecting. Protensive salespeople allow image enhancements to become exaggerated and distorted into *lifestyles*. Enhancements such as appearance, name dropping, cars, cameras and watches become *ends in themselves*. By emphatically displaying the symbols of success, protensive salespeople become immersed in the charade of accomplishment. To criticize or ignore any element of this charade is likely to be interpreted as a personal attack. Thus, simply offering advice can be seen as an attempt to scratch their veneer of accomplishment. Does this describe you?

Above Average?

Salespeople with protensive call reluctance are driven to seek out new ways to distance themselves from other salespeople, a race they consider to be inferior and which they sometimes hold in secret contempt.

To them, *other* salespeople hustle, whereas *they* market. *Others* prospect for new business, whereas *they* hold out for quality rather than quantity. Consequently, they initiate fewer numbers of contacts with prospective buyers (often alarmingly few), a practice which they defend with an allusion to large pie-in-the-sky cases which are always around the proverbial corner.

As a matter of personal principle, some insist on trying to circumvent prospecting altogether. To them, prospecting is a demeaning and unprofessional activity which plagues the path of other salespeople. Thus, some spend their prospecting time trying to discover how to get prospective clients to come to them. Others cover by investing their time, energy and money in the ceremonial dance of professionalism: Instead of initiating contact with prospective clients, they join professional organizations, climb their political ranks, and behave with the solemnity of a valedictorian at a high school graduation. Some write books. Others get on the speaking circuit. Few prospect. None readily admit to being call reluctant.

Critical Reflexes

If you have protensive call reluctance, you probably try to avoid objective self-evaluation and may have a history of discrediting the people and procedures that could offer help.

Are you a master dabbler in the enlightenments of our time? Do you consider yourself fluent in the jargon of abstract mentalism? Do you find yourself reciting a running commentary on behavior change techniques instead of seriously trying to apply them to yourself?

If you answer "yes" to any of the above questions, you probably have *tried* them all: role playing, mind control, biofeedback, sensitivity training, Est, Neurolinguistic Programming, Transactional Analysis, and all the other attempts to explain the irony and complexity of the human experience. Your exposure to these programs probably followed a predictable pattern. First, you took small doses over a very short time. Second, you failed to adhere to instructions or complete assignments. Third, you concluded that the program was not effective and reduced it to just another disappointment. Right? The procedure was shallow, or the practitioner was misguided, or the time was just not right for *you* to change. It never is. So you predictably dropped out, unenlightened and unchanged.

Exit Ramp Number One

The above rituals are common to protensive call reluctance; it's how you have been coping up to now, unsuccessfully. Maybe this time will be different, maybe it won't. But if you are going to drop out again, read no further and do it now. It's your choice.

On Being Right

Congratulations. Since you are still reading, we assume that you have decided to go toe-to-toe with the urge to drop out. Most salespeople with protensive call reluctance don't make the choice you just made. Regrettably, most don't get any further than the last part of the last paragraph. Here's why.

Salespeople with protensive call reluctance listen and read on two levels. One level is fueled by curiosity plus a genuine desire to perform at peak performance levels. This is what has brought you to this point.

Operating at a second, more subtle level is the part of you that fears self-promotion. It works to keep you at a safe distance from the content and purpose of books like this one. It will bog you down with petty nit-picking, compulsive fault-finding, and involuntary critical commentary *about* what you read *while* you are reading it. Then it will discredit the content and persuade you against taking it seriously. And since the content is not considered worthwhile, you are relieved from any practical obligation to try it.

If you will objectively observe yourself for a moment, you may notice that you have been evaluating what you have been reading. You are probably doing it *right now*. But grant us the use of one platitude: In the battle with protensive call reluctance, *being right is the booby prize.*

Risking

The tendency to deflect personal responsibility for call reluctance is the primary reason that your corrective efforts usually fail regardless of which procedure is being used or who is applying it. So the first step to overcome protensive call reluctance is to take a risk. If your prospecting activity is below what you know your ability to be, then you must assume personal responsibility for not performing at your capable level and make an effort to do something meaningful about it.

It's a *risk*. You may succeed or you may fail. But the act of trying will level the first deafening blow to your call reluctance by reaffirming your ability to *allow yourself to try*. Risking growth is an act of personal strength which defies the infantile part of you which has successfully asserted up to now that you could never be afraid *and* prospect, never be afraid *and* survive.

Exit Ramp Number Two

Fear Inversion begins with four agreements you make with yourself. Each should be considered carefully.

Agreement Number One: Do you agree to recognize that your prospecting is not consistent with your level of ability? Yes or no?

Agreement Number Two: Do you agree to temporarily suspend your tendency to blame, criticize or make excuses for your call reluctant behavior? Yes or no?

Agreement Number Three: Will you honestly make an effort to do something significant about your call reluctance other than just thinking or talking about it? Yes or no?

Agreement Number Four: Do you agree to follow our instructions completely and in the order they are given without demanding any explanations? Yes or no?

Can you allow yourself to agree? If you can agree to these terms, you are ready to proceed to a mysterious but effective process you should find helpful. If you cannot or will not agree to the terms, then stop reading at this point and turn instead to a less demanding self-help source which will be less threatening. (Be careful. Your decision will either be made by choice or by default. Continuing to read or skim beyond this point without agreeing or responding to the terms above, psychologically invalidates this procedure for you because it interprets your answers to be "no.")

FEAR INVERSION DAY-BY-DAY

Days One and Two

The first two days of Fear Inversion are devoted to learning to follow instructions. This will be done by unplugging your critical reflex circuit. You will use a simplified form of Thought Zapping. Begin by placing a rubber band on your left wrist. Whenever you find yourself about to criticize, add to, modify or amend in any way what you read, or what people say to you, sting your wrist while imagining yourself yelling "Stop it!" as loud as you can. Unless you derive pleasure from pain, your reflexive criticality is about to enter the last two days of its life.

Does this mean you should never criticize? No, it just means you will not do it as a *lifestyle*, automatically and all the time, as a *covering maneuver*. Your criticisms will become more authentic since they will be made out of choice, not rigid habit.

Day Three

Watch out for *understanding*. The compulsion to understand everything about protensive call reluctance can get you into serious trouble. Dance around it. It's a booby trap. Though the path to understanding *looks* productive, interesting and beguiling, be warned, for it boasts a high body count among salespeople with protensive call reluctance. You do not have to understand everything about protensive call reluctance in order to change. You already know if you have it and probably already understand much about why. Your lack of success is due to your not doing anything productive about it.

Begin this day's activities by examining your Fear Cycle. Concentrate on what you actually *do* in reaction to your fears about prospecting. But think about what you do simply as an inefficient *action*. Try not to think of it as a symptom, problem or imperfection. It's not. It's just what you do under certain circumstances. Describe it nonjudgmentally. Think about what you do, though it won't be easy. But don't fight it. Allow the part of you that fears (humiliation, exposure or whatever) the right to censor your answer. When it senses that the time is right, your recollection of what you do when you are afraid will float to the surface of your consciousness. When it does, copy it on a piece of paper. Here's an example:

> "When I try to prospect. . .I guess I do get a little defensive and hostile."

Now rewrite your answer in terms of your behavior. For example, "I get defensive and hostile" really means:

> "I get belligerent with my trainer and argue that prospecting is unprofessional."

Day Four

Following, we have provided a list of short questions for you to answer during today's activities. The questions are about prospecting. When you are alone at home or in your office, stand in front of a full length mirror. *Verbally* ask the questions one at a time to your image in the mirror. Then answer each one as completely and honestly as you can. Spend at least five minutes, preferably more, answering each question. As you answer each question, allow the critic in you to take control. Notice your image in the mirror. How are you standing? How does your voice sound? How do you look? Are your answers really honest and sound? *Make yourself find fault with what you see and hear, and verbally criticize as much as you can.*

This activity can be even more effective if it is video taped. If you video tape the activity, first record your spontaneous answers to the questions without criticism. Then play the tape back and make yourself criticize what you see and hear.

Questions to ask yourself:

- Where are you when you experience call reluctance?

- What exactly are you doing when your call reluctance begins?

- How long do you tend to continue behaving this way once it begins?

- What do you feel?

- Could you make yourself feel it more on Tuesdays than on Thursdays?

- Does your call reluctance feel the same when you are dressed in a blue shirt or blouse as it does when you are dressed in a white shirt or blouse?

- What mental images do you see?

- What are the usual reasons you give for behaving this way (fear of rejection, etc.)?

- Do you *really* want to change this behavior? Yes or no?

If you answered the last question "yes," you are probably being too uncritical. If you answered "no," you have taken a risk by being very forthright with yourself and have clearly demonstrated that you are prepared to continue to the next section.

Day Five

Why are you reading this book? Most people give very general reasons for wanting to improve or correct something within themselves. But we would like you to be as focused as possible on the outcomes you desire for yourself. You need to state your goal in your *own* language and in terms that are meaningful to you, and which you can dedicate yourself to. For example, instead of just saying, "I want to stop being call reluctant," you could say, "I want to stop feeling so *demeaned* when I try to make prospecting phone calls." Or, you could say that you wanted to stop critically jumping on people and discrediting what they say before they finish saying it. As a general rule, your outcome should be stated in terms of a behavior as opposed to an idea, concept or virtue such as to "be a better salesperson."

So take a look at the examples below and decide what you would consider a successful outcome for you.

- To never fear prospecting again
- To reduce the frequency of call reluctance episodes
- To lower the intensity of call reluctance episodes when they occur
- To recognize that call reluctance episodes may occur, but learn to tolerate them better
- To be call reluctant only if and when I want to be
- To decrease the duration of call reluctance episodes

Based on the information above, decide what conditions must be met in order for you to consider this process a success. The process cannot continue indefinitely, so be sure to include a cutoff date. For example, "If by the end of six days I have at least improved based on the conditions I established above, then I consider the enterprise to have been successful." The termination date can be any reasonable length, but it should be no fewer than six days.

Day Six

Spend the sixth day reviewing what you have done in the past to cope with your call reluctance. Some salespeople forget their sales script in order to avoid having to recite it. Some become overly apologetic and passive when initiating contact with prospective buyers. Others conceal their fear by defensively lashing out with face-saving arguments. Some feel faint. Some protect themselves by imposing a cynical and sarcastic wall between them and their prospecting. What do you do? (Hint: The answer should be apparent in the critical conversation you had with yourself on the fourth day.)

Day Seven

Devote the seventh day to resistance. Let your mind wander (do not force it) to as many excuses as you can think of for dropping out now and refusing to seriously continue this procedure. It's not necessary to write down all your excuses but it would be helpful. It is necessary, however, to keep a running total of how many excuses come to mind during the course of the day. Begin your list by selecting at least two excuses from the list below. This should help you get started. Write all of your excuses on a small piece of paper and carry it with you in your wallet for the entire day.

- It's superficial.
- The authors have never sold anything themselves.
- The authors have never had call reluctance.
- Everybody has call reluctance, so why shouldn't I?
- Having call reluctance is my prerogative.
- It won't work anyway, nothing will.
- Even if it does work, it won't last.
- I'll look like a fool if I try.
- It will destroy my positive attitude.

Day Eight

The next prescription may strike you as preposterous, but remember your agreement to follow instructions. Refer back to day six. How do you cope with your call reluctance? Forgetting? Feeling faint? Arguing? Cynicism? Today you should really be *yourself.* At every appropriate opportunity, you are to mimic and exaggerate the way you have ineffectively coped with your call reluctance in the past. Really ham it up. Get into it. Make it real.

If you feel demeaned by having to make prospecting phone calls, then make several intensely demeaning calls. Feel really demeaned.

If you tend to lash out at and argue with your managers, then today do so *intentionally.* Try to create arguments. Try to keep a straight face while being intensely hostile.

If you tend to be uncoachable, create situations in which you can act like you already know everything. Refuse to be advised, counseled or trained. Act haughty. Know it all.

Day Nine

On the ninth day, tell at least one person who you do not particularly like or trust that you have been reading this book and trying out one of the procedures. Using all of the negative points in the list below, explain to them that the procedure does not work and the book is not worth reading. Be as convincing as possible. You can set the record straight after you have completed all of your activities.

- You have tried all the procedures in this book. None work.

- You have never really been call reluctant.

- Call reluctance can't penetrate your positive attitude.

- You are pretending to be call reluctant just to be able to try a procedure in this book.

As you can see, this procedure is not meant for everyone. It takes a certain amount of imagination to make it work. But if you have honored the agreements you made with yourself and followed the instructions as given, at least some results should be evident by now.

Negative thought habits which produce distressful feelings during prospecting can be eliminated if they can be stopped in their course. And they can.

R̖ FIVE

THOUGHT ZAPPING

PRIMARILY AFFECTS:

X Thoughts

X Feelings

  Actions

PRESCRIBED FOR:

X Threat Sensitivity
X Desurgency
X Protension
X Groups
  Personal Friends
  Disruption Sensitivity
  Social Differential
  Role Acceptance
  Family/Relatives

A BRIEF OVERVIEW

Each day, when you first look at yourself in the mirror, you make a fundamental choice: "Will I allow myself to be *satisfied* or *dissatisfied* with what I see?" The choice made by self-limiting people usually reflects mindless negative thought habits which ignore the objective image in the mirror. Some salespeople who are motivated and goal-directed are unable to prospect for much the same reason. Their prospecting efforts are consistently blocked by mindless negative concerns which must be forced aside, at considerable cost, each time they approach certain prospecting situations.

Thought Zapping can help. It is direct, fast, effective and easy to apply. It works by interrupting the *habitual* thoughts which precede unpleasant *feelings* about prospecting. With sledge hammer subtly, guided interruptions sever the critical link which connects negative concerns to negative feelings.

Guiding Principles Behind Thought Zapping

1. You are *motivated* to overcome call reluctant reactions to prospecting.

2. Your motivation is *directed* specifically towards reducing unwanted distressful feelings associated with self-promotion in order to improve your prospecting activity.

3. Feelings can enhance or impede the flow of motivation into goal-directed behavior.

4. Habits are strengthened by uninterrupted repetition.

5. Habits are weakened by interruption.

Sighting the Target

Thought Zapping is useful for correcting certain types of the fear of self-promotion. It is best suited to those forms of call reluctance—Threat Sensitivity, Desurgency, Protension and Groups—which consist of *generalized* fear. Because Thought Zapping is easy to learn and produces fast results when properly applied, it has been a popular procedure at the Call Reluctance Center.

Estimated Completion Time

Weakening the habitual connection between unwanted thoughts and unwanted feelings can usually be accomplished within about five days.

THE ROLE OF HABITS

Habits play important supporting roles in our lives. They help make certain complex and repetitive acts such as driving, walking and various social courtesies possible without having to constantly stop and think about them. Habits make our lives more enjoyable.

But some renegade habits can make our lives miserable. Habits of thought and feeling, like certain forms of the fear of self-promotion, can remain active long after they have served their self-protecting purpose. These habits do little more than frustrate, perplex and annoy us.

Have you ever driven a car for a period of time with a manual transmission and then tried to drive an automatic? By habit, your leg muscles try to push down on the clutch pedal only to find the brake instead. In the meantime, your hand reaches for a nonexistent stick shift. Retraining ourselves to adjust to an automatic transmission once we have become accustomed to a manual one takes practice and purposeful effort.

At first, the transition feels awkward. But by *suppressing* the old habits and repeating, forcibly if necessary, the new behaviors, the old habits soon loosen their iron grip. This method also works with habits of thought and feeling. By repeatedly interrupting yourself whenever an unwanted behavior asserts itself, and substituting the desired behavior in its place, an old habit dies and a new habit is born. That is how Thought Zapping works.

Breaking the Bond

Negative thought habits which produce distressful feelings can be eliminated if they can be stopped in their course. And they can, as the following exercise demonstrates.

Get a clock radio and tune to the most annoying station you can find. Turn the volume up loud. Now set it to go off in three minutes. Find a comfortable place to sit in a quiet room and place the radio nearby. Sit down. Close your eyes. Allow yourself to ponder the most fearful situation you can think of which is not related to prospecting. Really get into it and stay with it until the radio signals that your three minutes are up. ACTION BREAK.

What happened? If you are like most salespeople, several interesting things occurred. We ambiguously asked you to "ponder," so how did you carry out the instructions? What did you actually do? You probably "thought about" the most fearful thing you could recall which was not related to prospecting. But *how* did you do that?

Everyone can recall a particularly distressful memory. But most salespeople do not immediately recall distressful feelings. Instead, they begin by *searching* through the dusty, cluttered files of their mind for a *picture, smell* or *sound* which is *connected by a habit of memory* to a distressful feeling which, *once identified, they then feel*. (By "feel" we mean to actually *reexperience*, not just recall.)

The connection between what we *recall* and how we emotionally *react* is essentially one of habit. The habit is strong because each time we recall a particular event we immediately reexperience the same feelings. Through repetition, the connection between the two becomes formidable. But is it unbreakable? No.

Think about the experiment you just conducted. What happened as you sat with your eyes closed, got into your disturbing event, and felt the distressful feelings which accompanied it? Three minutes passed and the radio came on. As it did, the bond uniting your memory to your feelings was momentarily *interrupted*. A new experience was introduced which interfered with the connection between the thought and the feeling. Were you momentarily startled when the radio came on? Did you shift you attention, for a second, *to the sound of the radio* and *away from* the distressful feelings you were reexperiencing? If you did, then Thought Zapping will work for you.

You cannot attend to external interference and internal memories *at the same time.* The survival of a habit rests upon the thin thread of uninterrupted repetition. A purposeful interruption is a bad habit's worst enemy.

Listing Your Negative Intruders

What habits of thought and feeling interfere with your ability to prospect? The following activity will help you find out. Take out a piece of paper and divide it into two columns. Title the top of the page Inventory of Negative Intruders. Title the first column Negative Thoughts and the second column Emotional Reactions. Carry your Inventory of Negative Intruders with you for at least one work day, preferably two or three. Every time you prepare to prospect (or are in the process of prospecting) list the negative thoughts and accompanying emotional reactions.

Here are some examples of Negative Intruders that the authors had to contend with prior to giving presentations before company conventions and other assemblies.

Inventory of Negative Intruders

Negative Thoughts	Emotional Reactions
Worry about gathering all possible documentation in support of presentation	Muscle tension
Worry about the questions which might be asked	Dread
Worry about being late for a convention presentation	Agitation
Worry about how I look in front of a group	Compulsive shopping for new clothes
Worry about running over allotted time	Hurried

These are just some of the things we *habitually* worried about. Our worrying amounted to ineffective coping which sapped energy from our goals without returning a single ounce of relief. We applied Thought Zapping to ourselves and it worked. It can work for you too.

Recording the Negative Intruders

The next step is important and should be performed right after you have completed your inventory. You will need a lined tablet. Title the first page, Frequency of Intrusion Chart: Pre. Under the title, list any one of the intruding negative thoughts from your inventory. We recommend that you begin with one of the least distressful thoughts. Then set up the remainder of the page as shown below. What you should have when you finish is an intrusive negative thought you wish to zap, the date your measurement is taken, the time span the measurement covers, and a place for the total number of times the negative thought occurs during the measurement period.

Frequency of Intrusion Chart: Pre

Intruding Negative Thought (From Inventory Of Negative Thought Intruders): "Worry about the questions which might be asked" _____

_____

_____

Date: 11/5/83   Measurement Period: 8 hours

Occurrence During Measurement Period: 11 times

To get your total, simply keep track of the number of times the negative thought comes to mind (intrudes) during the time period you have selected. Then simply total it and copy it onto a form set up like the one above.

Zapping the Intruder

Now that you have discovered how often the negative thought intrudes, you are ready to do something about it.

One: Begin by placing a rubber band around your left wrist. It should be large enough to fit loosely.

Two: Sit in a comfortable chair and close your eyes.

Three: Think about the intruder you selected. Every time you become aware of the negative thought, do the following:

- Imagine the sky turning into a huge *stop sign*.

- As you see the stop sign, imagine yourself shouting, *"Stop it!"* as loud as you can.

- Simultaneously *snap* the rubber band and sting your wrist. Yes, it hurts. Once you begin this program, it is imperative to sting yourself *every time* you have the negative thought. Wherever you are. Whatever you are doing.

- Immediately after snapping the rubber band, think of a positive mental picture of yourself. For example, you might recall a time when you did well in a similar situation and felt good about yourself afterwards. Remember that event and allow yourself to reexperience some of those good feelings. If you can't think of anything, then allow yourself to pretend.

- Now, while reexperiencing these *pleasant* sensations, momentarily place yourself mentally back into the negatively intrusive situation you are trying to defang.

Now that you are familiar with Thought Zapping, you will find it easy to transfer to real life situations. Every time your negative thought about prospecting intrudes, *zap it, insert* positive sensations, and *monitor* the number of times the thought intrudes on your post chart illustrated below. Within a few days, you will notice a significant decline in the frequency with which the negative thought intrudes.

You may only have to actually use the rubber band during your treatment of the first negative intruder. After two or three days of practice, it can be removed. Your *memory* of the rubber band's effect will linger far after its removal, and from this point on the phrase, "Stop it!" will have developed its own potency.

Measuring Your Progress

You can monitor your improvement by completing the Frequency of Intrusion Chart: Post (see below) which is set up like the Frequency of Intrusion Chart: Pre. Use it to track the frequency of your intruders once you begin Thought Zapping. By using it, you can observe your daily progress.

Frequency of Intrusion Chart: Post

Intruding Negative Thought (From Inventory Of Negative Thought Intruders): _____

_____

_____

Date:_____   Measurement Period:____

Occurrence During Measurement Period:_____

Is Thought Zapping the Same as Positive Thinking?

It would be reasonable to ask if Thought Zapping is not just another, more modern form of positive thinking.

No. Positive thinking and other methods like it stress positive mental imagery and rely on sheer repetition to establish new habits of positive thought. They assume that this process will eventually lead to more positive behavior.

Thought Zapping concentrates on *eliminating* the negative stumbling blocks which keep salespeople from being able to successfully think positively. The use of positive imagery is secondary.

The link between positive images alone and observable productive behavior has yet to be clearly evidenced except through anecdotal reports.

The link between Thought Zapping and the successful elimination of unwanted behavior can be easily measured by almost anyone willing to apply the procedure correctly and complete the pre and post forms.

Positive Thinking is essentially *semantic*. It relies on the use of words and often appeals to highly subjective concepts such as the "unconscious mind" to explain otherwise unexplainable behavior and thought.

Thought Zapping is essentially an objective, mechanical procedure. It disrupts and punishes self-limiting habits, thereby decreasing the frequency of their occurrence.

Breaking the Fear of Groups

When Gail B came to the Call Reluctance Center she had already survived beyond the norm for her industry. She had been in direct sales for 36 marginally productive months. Although her training was only minimal and her support from management superficial, she knew that she had what was necessary to do extraordinarily well. But she admitted to one nagging problem, call reluctance.

During the initial intake interview, Gail said she was in cosmetics sales with a highly visible company using the "party" concept for prospecting and selling. The Call Reluctance Scale (SPQ test) revealed that Gail had a vulnerability to call reluctance, but only in one form, *speaking in front of groups.* Having that fear made it difficult not only for her to speak in front of groups but also to set up the number of parties needed to meet her production objectives.

Gail had previously been exposed to a variety of potential cures, but each had failed and she became somewhat cynical. Yet beneath the cynicism, she still had a strong desire to improve.

Gail, an action-oriented salesperson, consented to try Thought Realignment although we suspected that because of her cynicism it would prove to be more helpful in the future. As expected, Thought Realignment failed to dazzle her with immediate results, but she persevered and was soon ready for the next prescription, Thought Zapping.

Expecting another *mental* approach, Gail was very receptive to the practical, straightforward nature of Thought Zapping. We demonstrated the procedure by having her close her eyes and concentrate on her problem. Shortly, we interrupted by shouting "Stop it, Gail!" Convinced that this would work for her version of call reluctance, she completed her setup charts listing several other intruders.

Gail chose to start her strategy with the first intrusion on her list, "Having to speak before a group of women makes me feel so exposed and vulnerable, I can't concentrate on my presentation." Using her Frequency of Intrusion Chart: Pre, she found that her negative thought interfered *every* time she tried to use a contact to set up a party. During a typical day, she recorded the intruder each time it occurred and discovered that it appeared at the rate of 17 times per hour.

Gail was then given the rubber band. To be sure that she knew how to use it correctly, we had her imagine getting ready to call a contact to set up a party while becoming aware of the intruder and zapping it before the accompanying negative feeling could occur. Then, instead of the usual negative feeling, we had her visualize herself setting up a previous party *she had found to be enjoyable. She reexperienced the enjoyable sensations.*

At first Gail reacted with the usual litany, "This hurts! My wrist will develop welts. I'll look like some kind of junkie! Visualizing is phoney. It's not really me. Isn't there some other way?" Without arguing with her, we secured her commitment to continue the procedure.

She went out into her world of prospecting with her rubber band and monitor forms. Although her next clinic appointment was a week away, she called our office two days later. She no longer needed the rubber band or the next appointment. It hurt but it worked. Fast. She could now prospect without the intrusion of the first negative thought and was already working on the next thought on her list. Thought Zapping worked for Gail. She has developed into a powerful prospector and is really enjoying herself in the process.

A Final Remark

Sometimes old habits do not die and remain buried. They sometimes resurface to haunt again, though to a lesser degree. So be prepared. The old habit may occasionally try to reassert itself. The phenomenon is called spontaneous recovery. It's natural. You can expect it. When it happens, don't panic. Just reach for your rubber band and give yourself a booster shot.

Thought Zapping is a fast way to develop new habits of thought and feeling. It is fast, but it is not instant. Give it the time, attention and patience that your particular application deserves.

3

THE
RESEARCH

Though far from perfect, the relationship between call reluctance and sales performance is more predictable than the daily fluctuations in the Dow Jones Average or weather forecasts three days in the future.

CHAPTER FOUR

CALL RELUCTANCE RESEARCH

RESEARCH ON THE FEAR OF SELF-PROMOTION

The staff of the Call Reluctance Center are compulsive people-watchers. We watch all types of people in all kinds of settings. Some have call reluctance and some do not. Our observations have taken us to uncharted fields of human enterprise where, hidden in the researcher's version of a duck hunter's blind, we have had the opportunity to use our eyes, ears and highly specialized test instruments to observe many talented people caught in their own mental traps. But unlike the hunter, we do not observe for sport or entertainment. We measure and graph, calculate and classify so that we and other professionals can do a better job helping people escape the lures and traps of unintentional career self-destruction.

For example, two of our studies strongly suggest that the fear of self-promotion does not only assume the form of call reluctance and limit the careers of direct salespeople. In the data processing environment, we found that post-training supervisory ratings of technical competence were highly influenced by personality variables associated with self-promotion. In a recent study, we found that over a five-year period, the number of promotions and salary increases in home office administrative personnel was significantly correlated to only one personality factor, *the willingness to self-promote.*

Which Type of Call Reluctance is Most Common?

Call reluctance is a form of the fear of self-promotion which limits the prospecting activity of salespeople. But which type occurs most frequently?

People unaided by objective measurement tend to see the world in ways they are familiar and comfortable with. Their observations are interpreted to fit their experiences, expectations and values. For example, one sales selection consultant, who himself is highly protensive, actually *recommends* candidates with extremely *high* protension scores for sales positions. Sales managers who themselves have family call reluctance believe that type to be the most common. Popular thinking among salespeople, and people in general, is that group call reluctance is the most prevalent. Senior sales and marketing executives are sure that their efforts are being continuously thwarted by social differential call reluctance. But which type is *really* the most common?

No categorical statement can be safely made about which type is most common due to wide variations that exist across industries and even across departments within the same company. The following chart profiles the incidence of call reluctance in two sales offices of the same company located in the same geographic area. Although the total call reluctance in both operations is about the same, the types vary significantly.

Type of Call Reluctance	Locality "A"	Locality "B"
Threat Sensitivity	3.50	3.50
Desurgency	4.00	3.75
Protension	3.00	4.50
Groups	4.75	3.00
Friends	1.50	3.50
Role Acceptance	4.00	3.25
Disruption Sensitivity	5.75	3.30
Social Differential	6.50	2.75
Family	.50	1.25
Total Call Reluctance	33.50	28.80

Total call reluctance is measured on a 90-point scale. Individual types are measured on a 10-point scale. The *higher* the number, the more call reluctance is indicated.

While recognizing the need for information about specific sales operations, we can proceed to chart the most common types of call reluctance found in general and in some representative industries. (Data exists for many more, but space does not permit listing them all.)

Call Reluctance

Ranked by Overall Frequency of Occurrence

Type	Rank	Marker Behavior
Disruption Sensitivity	1	Fears being pushy
Desurgency	2	Over-prepares
Family	3	Fears loss of family approval

Friends	4	Fears losing friends
Protension	5	Fears being humiliated
Role Acceptance	6	Ashamed to be in sales
Social Differential	7	Fears being intimidated
Groups	8	Fears group presentations
Threat Sensitivity	9	Won't take social risks

Disruption Sensitivity, the fear of being seen by others as pushy or intrusive, is by far the most common type of call reluctance found in salespeople. Comparatively speaking, Threat Sensitivity is relatively rare. Characterized by outward signs such as shyness and social awkwardness, it is usually screened out by selection interviewers and tests. But this global mosaic is not nearly as interesting or informative as our more detailed observations of call reluctance types found in particular industries and selling environments.

Cross Cultural Studies

Our studies found stockbrokers to be more call reluctant overall than other professional sales groups. With the invaluable assistance of experienced professionals within this industry—Dr. Jerry Holmes with Rauscher, Pierce, Refsnes and Dr. Carolyn Bishop with Howard, Weil, Labouisse, Friedrichs—we were able to analyze valuable test data which corroborated our conclusion and pointed us to the next issue, most prevalent type. According to our studies, brokers as a group tend to be most predisposed to Protension, the fear of humiliation. They are vulnerable to a self-sabotaging fear that some current or prospective client might question their professional competence, or even their integrity. The second most frequent type of call reluctance observed in brokers is Disruption Sensitivity. Group and social differential call reluctance, common in some industries, have an unimportant influence on stockbrokers.

Bank trust officers, a profession that is new to competitive selling, are a different matter altogether. Residing in highly traditional, hierarchical organizations which must now compete for sales with more experienced sales-oriented financial service organizations, trust officers as a group tend to be highly susceptible to desurgent call reluctance. But this conclusion is more logical than surprising. Many come from *technical* backgrounds and did not anticipate becoming direct salespeople. Armed with extensive product knowledge but minimum sales training, they are now supposed to competitively prospect and sell. More than a few are having extreme difficulty doing either. Some look like they are suffering from combat fatigue.

Financial planners, another relatively new addition to the financial services industry, are also prone to desurgent call reluctance. Although we have analyzed call reluctance data from large samples, this conclusion is somewhat more tentative than some of our others. First, it is often difficult to determine what any new species is. With financial planners, it has proven to be *very* difficult. From our admittedly confused perspective, it appears that they are actually an amalgam of professionals from other sales disciplines such as banking, insurance and stockbrokering. Apparently, salespeople from these parishes can call themselves financial planners after having completed one or another specialized course of study. Most admit that they must prospect and close in order to get business. This qualifies them, in our judgement, as salespeople. A non-representative minority, however, insists that they do *not* sell, they do not prospect, and they do not collect a commission, which is providential since they definitely *do* have call reluctance. The majority, those who call *themselves* financial planning *salespeople*, are most vulnerable to desurgent call reluctance, a trait they share with trust officers and certain groups of manufacturer's reps, drug detailers and computer hardware salespeople.

The insurance industry is a moving target. Generalizations are especially dangerous here considering the contortions and traumatic changes this industry is experiencing. But some are possible, and one is inescapable: Call reluctance is and has traditionally been a particularly difficult problem for the insurance industry. In a recent magazine article, M.C. "Rusty" McGlasson, an insurance educator and regular contributor to *Life Insurance Selling*, one of the industry's most widely read periodicals, described call reluctance as the "social disease" of the insurance sales profession. We agree. We have found that regardless of what companies call their salespeople (financial planners, account executives, client representatives), Role Acceptance emerges to short circuit the sales function. This appears to be especially true in organizations where agents are given alternative *names* (financial planners, etc.) but initial training remains entirely focused on *insurance* sales. The result is a mixed message to agents which echoes across company affiliation, products sold or markets worked. Role Acceptance is characterized by an unverbalized nucleus of uncertainty, shame and guilt about career choice. It undoubtedly originates in the callous and insensitive stereotypes reflexively pinned on salespeople in that industry by the general public, and *often unintentionally by the industry itself.* Too often, when it first occurs as honest doubt and emotional unfinished business, sales managers maladaptively drive it underground with their indignant denials that stereotypes are a problem and their bursts of rapid-fire platitudes. Once underground, it ferments until it bursts.

Certain local agencies are noteworthy exceptions to the industry trend. Run by skilled and experienced managers, these operations make call reluctance a matter of serious attention. One such example is Dave Stewart, Mutual of Omaha's agency manager in Billings, Montana. Stewart has 30 agents, "21 of which are honor club producers." His agency boasts impressive production statistics in everything from mutual funds to life insurance. Retention, a perennial problem in the insurance industry, is exceptional. He has "won every contest we've been in." But Stewart's most startling accomplishment is that he did it all during his first year in Billings. It would be a mistake to attribute Mr. Stewart's success to either an act of fate or some other simple solution. According to him, his success was planned and the centerpiece of that plan was the proper management of call reluctance. Stewart made it a priority. It made a difference.

Some industries consist of companies which have built their strength on informal party sales. Our investigations in this sales setting have had the cooperation and guidance of executives from some of its key sales organizations such as Richard Reff, president of Home Galleries, one of the newest and most successful companies operating in the party sales arena. Common sense points to group call reluctance as one of the most troublesome types in this setting. But Reff thinks otherwise. He says family and friends call reluctance are particularly dangerous because salespeople in that industry must "begin with people they know" in order to succeed. He suspects that this holds true for other members of the Direct Sales Association as well.

Call reluctance also has a dramatic influence on real estate sales. But the impact shifts somewhat according to the type of real estate involved. People selling commercial real estate, for example, are inclined to be slightly more desurgent than residential salespeople. Their desurgency is innocuous most of the time. But it strikes a debilitating blow when cold calling is required. Salespeople in residential real estate appear prone to Disruption Sensitivity.

Our work with telemarketers has produced a curious and unexpected finding. They are more disruption sensitive than other sales groups. Hesitant to be considered intrusive, many can cope by prospecting and selling *on the phone* but would be unable to do the same face-to-face. Call reluctance data on telemarketers has come from many and varied sources. One of the most significant is Monex International. Monex has been selling gold and silver by phone for many years. Its sales force, headed by sales vice president Jack Tate, is one of the best managed operations of any type we have observed. Through management team leaders, Monex also places a priority on the management of call reluctance. Management

Call Reluctance Types by Industry

Industry	Most Frequent Type
Telemarketers	Disruption Sensitivity
General Sales Management	Desurgency
Computer Hardware	Desurgency
Stockbrokers	Protension
HRD Consultants/Trainers	Protension
Insurance	Role Acceptance
Business Machines	Social Differential
Real Estate, Commercial	Desurgency
Real Estate, Residential	Disruption Sensitivity
Financial Planners	Desurgency

team leaders approach the problem head-on in the company's sales training program. In an environment where Disruption Sensitivity could be devastating, team leaders are straightforward with their salespeople. "If I were asked to specify one single cause above all others for selling failure," teaches team leader Charley Rodriquez, "it would be call reluctance." But he doesn't stop there. A mixture of high tech measurement coupled with genuine concern and sound sales training help Monex effectively manage call reluctance.

Serious work with call reluctance is not limited to the United States. Interest in call reluctance research is growing steadily in other countries as well. The most influential and highly developed programs are found in Australia. There, under the direction of McCann Consultants, a leading Australian consulting firm in Brisbane, and Dr. Ted Leong, that firm's professional associate in Sydney, valuable research has been quietly and steadily progressing. The Call Reluctance Scale is being used to sample prospecting palpitations in a variety of Australian industries. Although there are some language and cultural differences, the results to date have been enlightening and encouraging. For example, they have learned that data processing representatives in large international companies operating in Australia are more vulnerable to protensive call reluctance than to other types. In that respect, they resemble their U.S. counterparts. McCann's group is particularly interested in the extent to which the various types of call reluctance influence actual sales performance. For example, by correlating the degree of protensive call reluctance found in data processing salespeople against the actual percent of annual sales quota achieved, the Australians have found that as protensive call reluctance goes *up*, sales production tends to go *down*. (In one study, the average attained annual sales quota for the three most call reluctant sales reps was 45%. Attained quota for the three reps with the lowest protensive call reluctance was 118%.) McCann's group also found a strong relationship between social differential call reluctance and sales performance in data processing sales reps. These results, from small but highly useful samples, provide additional evidence that the nine types of call reluctance are more than theory. They actually do influence sales performance.

In other studies, the Australians found that capital (heavy) equipment salespeople in that country also tend to be much like their counterparts in the U.S., with one exception. They tend to be slightly more desurgent. In the insurance industry, Australian home office personnel tend to show some of the same progress-obstructing behaviors (associated with protension and desurgency) which tied up needed innovations in certain U.S. insurance companies for so long.

Environmental Factors

Salespeople bring the predisposition to certain forms of call reluctance with them to the sales career. Other forms are acquired once they get there. For example, we have learned that the call reluctance found in local sales offices often mirrors the type present in local sales management. Apparently, technical content is not the only thing transferred through the sales training process; attitudes towards prospecting are also learned. Call reluctance attitudes found in management can influence bottom-line considerations such as the tenure of sales reps. A recent study of call reluctance attitudes in sales managers revealed an alarming relationship between protension in sales managers and the tenure of their salespeople. But sales managers overall are not protensive, they are desurgent. Many, especially in technical sales areas, unintentionally contaminate some of their most promising new salespeople with small doses of desurgent call reluctance. But when protensive call reluctance *is* found in sales managers and consultants, it can have a lethal influence on tenure. In our study we found that the average tenure of sales reps *increased* as protension in their sales managers *decreased*. Managers and consultants averaging 6.5 on the protension scale (out of a possible 10), tended to keep their new sales reps less than six months. Managers and consultants averaging low amounts of protension (only 3 on the 10-point protension scale) tended to keep their new recruits an average of almost 12 months. We know that call reluctance attitudes in sales managers can have a subtle effect on more than just prospecting. They can also influence retention. This is a potentially volatile discovery since training consultants taken as a group have the highest protension of any group we have observed.

We have also found that some highly respected sales training programs can transmit hidden call reluctance messages. More importantly, we are somewhat shocked and amazed to learn that sales training departments, which would not knowingly poison their salespeople with tainted meat, are failing to check the content of their sales training programs for call reluctance contamination. Well-intended programs often contain subtle call reluctance messages embedded within their content. In more than a few cases, we have found call reluctance detonators which were being emphasized in certain sales training material. Once exposed, salespeople who were not call reluctant soon learned how to be.

Companies utilizing highly inspirational, *feeling based* sales training approaches are spawning grounds for call reluctance. Those stressing technical sales fundamentals within a formal training program seem to produce less call reluctance than is typical for their respective industries.

Age

Call reluctance appears to be modestly influenced by age. Total call reluctance increases somewhat with age, suggesting that older, more established salespeople definitely are not immune to call reluctance. But recent studies are continuing to refine our understanding of this phenomenon. An even stronger relationship between call reluctance and *experience* has been observed. If this is confirmed, it will reduce the importance of age as an influence and provide compelling additional support for the hypothesis that certain forms of call reluctance are *acquired* through exposure over time to sales managers, trainers and consultants who are themselves call reluctant.

Sex

Popular literature is correct that men and women do vary in many significant ways, but call reluctance is not one of them. Our research has shown that women are slightly more inclined to have family and group call reluctance, but this slight difference between the sexes is not large enough to merit practical importance.

Impact on Sales Performance

If you think that uncorrected call reluctance could be having a negative impact on your sales performance, you're probably right. At least that's what our studies have found. Although performance specialists like Dr. Charles Clark correctly maintain that sales performance is the result of many influences such as motivation, intelligence, personal values and life planning, the role of call reluctance is that of the critical link. And though far from perfect, the relationship between call reluctance and sales performance is more predictable than daily fluctuations in the Dow Jones Average or weather forecasts three days in the future.

For example, the average number of new universal life cases (orders) submitted by a group of life insurance agents having the *highest* call reluctance scores was seven per month. Another group with the *lowest* call reluctance scores averaged in excess of ten new cases per month.

The average annual production rank for new telemarketers with high call reluctance scores was 38th. The rank for telemarketers with low call reluctance scores was 28th, more than ten points better.

Certain forms of call reluctance have their greatest impact on early performance. The second month cumulative earnings (commissions) of one sample of new sales reps selling to up-market clients illustrates the point. Those with low social differential call reluctance scores averaged more than $3,000. Those with high social differential scores averaged only $600 for the same time period.

In another study, we found that call reluctance scores can be used to help predict early performance as early as the end of the first month of tenure. This was shown by giving a test to prospective sales reps and then setting the scores aside. We later went back and looked at the scores of those who were ultimately hired on the basis of other information to see what, if anything, predicted their production at the end of the first month. Again, those with high social differential scores averaged only $260 by the end of their first month. But those with low scores on social differential averaged more than $2,500 during the same time period. Similar relationships have been observed between other types of call reluctance and early performance. We have even found strong and unexpected relationships between sales performance and family and friends call reluctance in sales environments where family members and personal friends are not even the market. This supports the notion that a broader dimension, the fear of self-promotion, is what is actually being measured.

Hopefully, the research base we have just sampled helps you see that call reluctance is not just another trendy idea developed by marketers to exploit the self-help dollar. It is very real. It has been around for a long time. During that time, it has stolen from companies and salespeople their energy, satisfaction and financial rewards. But from the knowledge yielded by research programs like those just reviewed, bold new blockades have been built which can now be positioned to neutralize call reluctance and stop it in its tracks.

ABOUT THE AUTHORS

George W. Dudley and Shannon L. Goodson's pioneering work on the fear of self-promotion is known world-wide. They have been considered the leading authorities on the fear of self-promotion and call reluctance ever since their technical research began to appear several years ago. With backgrounds in experimental science, research to them is not a hobby, it's a lifestyle.

Dudley has a bachelors degree in psychology from Baylor University and a Masters Degree in experimental psychology from North Texas State University. While in the U.S. Marine Corps, he served in Field Testing and Evaluation. For several years he directed the Field Testing and Research unit of a Fortune 500 firm. A productive author and researcher, Dudley is also a highly sought after featured speaker. Each year he is invited to speak to many professional groups ranging from life insurance sales managers to advanced professional training for practicing psychologists.

Shannon L. Goodson has a bachelor's degree in psychology and a Master's degree in organizational psychology from Lamar University. She is an experienced psychotherapist, researcher and counselor. As co-author of numerous articles and publications on the fear of self-promotion and call reluctance, she has been regularly invited to present her research to academic and business organizations.

Although well known for their breakthrough research on the fear of self-promotion, they are even more at home as authors and researchers in the sub-speciality of personality and performance measurement. Both have received many honors for their work. Today, they continue to research, write, teach and consult with major businesses and professional clients. In demand as featured speakers, the team receives frequent requests to lecture on their research and to conduct seminars and workshops for business and professional audiences nationwide.

Personal Appearances

Authors/researchers George W. Dudley and Shannon L. Goodson have become two of the most highly sought-after keynote speakers and seminar leaders in the nation. Corporate, academic and public conventions regularly spotlight their pioneering research on *How to Overcome the Fear of Self-Promotion* as a kick-off to major sales campaigns or to boost individual performance. For more information about scheduling personal appearances for your company or convention, you may contact the authors through the publisher.

George W. Dudley/Shannon L. Goodson
c/o The Behavioral Science Research Press
2695 Villa Creek, Suite 100
Dallas, Texas 75234
(214-243-8543)

About the Tests

Some of the specialized research instruments used to measure the fear of self-promotion are available to individuals, corporations and appropriately trained consultants. The tests presently available are:

The Call Reluctance Scale	Measures all nine forms of call reluctance
Athena*Graph	Measures 17 dimensions of personality
Sales Profiles Analysis	Forecasts sales performance
Selling Styles Profile Analysis	Detects Primary and Backup selling styles
Compatibility Profile Analysis	Charts the probable working relationship between a sales manager/trainer and salesperson.

Tests may be administered by paper-and-pencil and sent to the publisher for evaluation or by state-of-the-art micro computer software which produces each of the reports listed above on site. (Note: The test software system is available to sales managers, corporate sales training departments, and certified consultants only.) Contact the Call Reluctance Center for prices and procedures if you wish to take the tests or would like more information about the self-contained micro computer testing software.

AUTHORS REQUEST FEEDBACK

How has the fear of self-promotion limited your career? What procedures did you apply before reading this book? Which techniques in this book worked best? The authors invite you to share your experiences with them. Your comments will help to encourage and guide them as they continue to refine their current methods, and develop new ones.

Address your comments to:

George W. Dudley & Shannon L. Goodson
c/o The Behavioral Science Research Press
2695 Villa Creek, Suite #100
Dallas, Texas 75234
FAX: (214)-243-6349

APPENDIX
SAMPLE REPORTS

Call Reluctance Scale for EXAMPLE A RUN CONTROL

	RAW SCORES	CONTRAST NORMS*	GEN'L NORMS
Presence / Severity			
==== BRAKE =========== XXXXXXXXXXXXX	47	35	45
==== ACCELERATOR ===== XXXXXXXXXXXX	43	55	45

Type(s) or Predisposition(s)
```
                --1--2--3--4--5--6--7--8--9-10
```

		RAW SCORES	CONTRAST NORMS*	GEN'L NORMS
THREAT SENSITIVITY . .	XXXXXXXXXXXX	4	3	5
DESURGENCY	XXXXXXXXXXXXXXXXXXXXXX	7	5	5
PROTENSION	XXXXXXXXXXXXXXXXXX	6	6	5
GROUP	XXXXXXXXXXXXXXX	5	4	5
FRIENDS	XXXXXXXXXXXXXXXXX	6	5	5
ROLE	XXXXXXXXX	3	2	5
DISRUPTION SENSITIVITY	XXXXXXXXXXXXXXX	5	5	5
SOCIAL DIFFERENTIAL .	XXXXXXXXXXXX	4	1	5
FAMILY	XXXXXXXXXXXXXXXXXXXXX	7	4	5

```
                --1--2--3--4--5--6--7--8--9-10
```
* Contrast Norms are for Experienced Stock Brokers

Critical Items Listing
6 critical question/answer combinations were observed.

I prefer a professional sales training program that :
Does not require salespersons to telephone or visit prospects who do not wish
to be contacted.

I would estimate that during the initial phases of my sales training it would
be appropriate to make sales calls on :
0% - 20% of my personal friends.

I prefer a sales training program that encourages salesmen and women to be
non-intrusive as opposed to training programs that encourage salespeople to
make EVERY possible sale.
True.

I would appreciate a sales training program that included a special section
devoted to learning how to use my personal friends as sales prospects.
False, because some of my friends might be justifiably offended if I made a
sales call on them, and professionally trained salespersons rarely - if ever
- resort to using their own friends as sales prospects.

Some people do not think very highly of sales people. Without disputing the
validity of their position, estimate how many people probably hold this view.
One out of three adults.

Salespeople, in my opinion, should be cautious about approaching members of
their own family as sales prospects, and should do so - if at all - only as a
LAST resort.
I strongly agree.

```
                    OVERVIEW
                    ========
This candidate's answers to SPQ questions indicate considerably more than
usual hesitation to initiate self-promotional contact in a variety of
situations. This could translate into job-related emotional distress, and
an insufficient number of contacts to sustain personal or career objectives.

                    Desurgency
                    ==========
     Individuals scoring high in this area tend to approach the task of
prospecting very cautiously, because it is important that they be perceived
as serious and knowledgeable professionals. They do not express feelings
easily and 'warm' to new people very slowly.
     Consequently, it tends to take them considerably longer to feel
comfortable with prospecting, because of the amount of preparation they
FEEL they must do before they have the emotional right to make a call on a
potential client. Therefore watch for excessive time spent in the office
acquiring technical knowledge versus time spent setting up appointments.
     This type of call-reluctance is easy to predict and prevent, moderately
easy to correct, and difficult to diagnose.

                Social Differential
                ===================
     Individuals scoring high in this area are afraid to call upon
professionals, such as accountants, attorneys, doctors, or anyone who they
perceive to be socio-economically better off than they are. Typically, they
will call on anyone but these individuals and can be quite successful until
it becomes necessary that they upgrade their business contacts. This type
of call-reluctance is difficult to predict, moderately easy to prevent, and
easy to diagnose and correct.

                    Family
                    ======
     Individuals falling into this category find it extremely difficult if
not impossible to call on personal relatives. They fear that they would be
jeopardizing their family by mixing business with their personal lives.
This type of call-reluctance is difficult to predict and prevent, and
moderately difficult to diagnose and correct.


          *   *   *   END  OF  REPORT   *   *   *
```

Behavioral Science Research Press

DATE: 10/17/85

NAME: SAMPLE, JOE

****

ATHENA*GRAPH OBJECTIVE PROFILE ANALYSIS

Copyright 1983,
THE BEHAVIORAL SCIENCE RESEARCH PRESS.
ALL RIGHTS RESERVED.
This report is intended to be confidential.
Reproduction of this report is prohibited.

BEHAVIORAL DIMENSIONS

```
RELATING:          0  1  2  3  4  5  6  7  8  9 10      STEN SCORE
People             *************                            4
Ideas              ******************                       6
------------------------------------------------------------------------------
LEARNING:          0  1  2  3  4  5  6  7  8  9 10      STEN SCORE
Conceptual         ********************                     6
Concrete           *************                            4
------------------------------------------------------------------------------
REACTIVITY:        0  1  2  3  4  5  6  7  8  9 10      STEN SCORE
Composed           **********************                   7
Excitable          **********                               3
------------------------------------------------------------------------------
DIRECTIVITY:       0  1  2  3  4  5  6  7  8  9 10      STEN SCORE
Forceful           ********************                     6
Yielding           *************                            4
------------------------------------------------------------------------------
EXPRESSIVENESS:    0  1  2  3  4  5  6  7  8  9 10      STEN SCORE
Expansive          *******                                  2
Restrained         ************************                 8
------------------------------------------------------------------------------
SELF-REGULATION:   0  1  2  3  4  5  6  7  8  9 10      STEN SCORE
Planful            **************************               9
Flexible           ****                                     1
------------------------------------------------------------------------------
VIGILENCE:         0  1  2  3  4  5  6  7  8  9 10      STEN SCORE
Adventurous        ***************************              9
Guarded            ****                                     1
------------------------------------------------------------------------------
SENSITIVITY:       0  1  2  3  4  5  6  7  8  9 10      STEN SCORE
Empathetic         ****                                     1
Rational           ***************************              9
------------------------------------------------------------------------------
PERCEPTION:        0  1  2  3  4  5  6  7  8  9 10      STEN SCORE
Skeptical          *******************                      6
Trusting           *************                            4
------------------------------------------------------------------------------
PERSPECTIVE:       0  1  2  3  4  5  6  7  8  9 10      STEN SCORE
Idealistic         ******************                       6
Practical          *************                            4
------------------------------------------------------------------------------
SOCIAL POISE:      0  1  2  3  4  5  6  7  8  9 10      STEN SCORE
Refined            **********                               3
Uncomplicated      *********************                    7
------------------------------------------------------------------------------
```

DATE: 10/17/85

NAME: SAMPLE, JOE

```
--------------------------------------------------------------------------------
OUTLOOK:            0  1  2  3  4  5  6  7  8  9 10      STEN SCORE
Concerned           ********************                      6
Optimistic          *************                             4
--------------------------------------------------------------------------------
CONVENTIONALITY:    0  1  2  3  4  5  6  7  8  9 10      STEN SCORE
Experimenting       ****************                          5
Traditional         ****************                          5
--------------------------------------------------------------------------------
RELIANCE:           0  1  2  3  4  5  6  7  8  9 10      STEN SCORE
Independent         *******************************          10
Collaborating       *                                         0
--------------------------------------------------------------------------------
FOCUS:              0  1  2  3  4  5  6  7  8  9 10      STEN SCORE
Purposeful          *******************************          10
Self-discovering    *                                         0
--------------------------------------------------------------------------------
ENERGY:             0  1  2  3  4  5  6  7  8  9 10      STEN SCORE
Intense             ********************                      6
Relaxed             *************                             4
--------------------------------------------------------------------------------
IMPRESSION:         0  1  2  3  4  5  6  7  8  9 10      STEN SCORE
Fluid               ****************                          5
Fixed               ****************                          5
--------------------------------------------------------------------------------
```

11:04:24
02-02-1986

SERVICE HOTLINE: 214-243-8543, M-F, DURING NORMAL WORKING HOURS

INDEX